P9-DDN-579

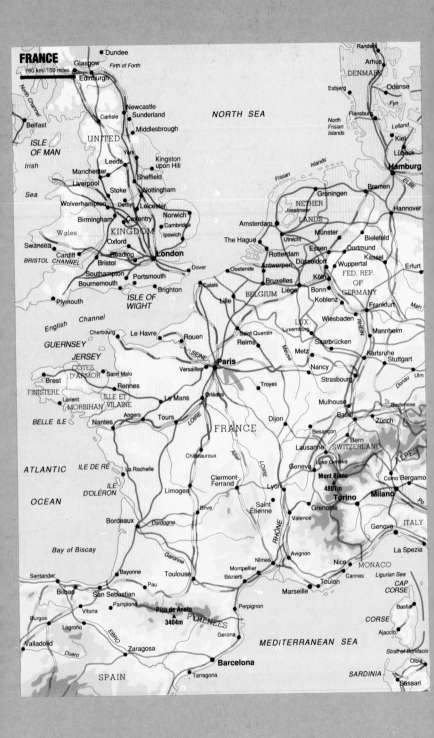

INSIGHT *pocket* GUIDES

PARIS

Written and Presented by **Grace Coston**

Grace Coston

INSIGHT
pocket
GUIDES

Insight Pocket Guide:

PaRIS

Directed by
Hans Höfer

Editorial Director
Andrew Eames

Photography by
Guy Bourdíer

Design Concept by
V. Barl

Design by
Karen Hoisington

© **1993 APA Publications (HK) Ltd**

All Rights Reserved

Printed in Singapore by
Höfer Press (Pte) Ltd
Fax: 65-8616438

Distributed in the United States by
Houghton Mifflin Company
2 Park Street
Boston, Massachusetts 02108
ISBN: 0-395-65753-9

Distributed in Canada by
Thomas Allen & Son
390 Steelcase Road East
Markham, Ontario L3R 1G2
ISBN: 0-395-65753-9

Distributed in the UK & Ireland by
GeoCenter International UK Ltd
The Viables Center, Harrow Way
Basingstoke, Hampshire RG22 4BJ
ISBN: 9-62421-505-7

Worldwide distribution enquiries:
Höfer Communications Pte Ltd
38 Joo Koon Road
Singapore 2262
ISBN: 9-62421-505-7

Bienvenue!

 Welcome! I have lived in Paris for 10 years, as a writer, translator and teacher, and can firmly say that I wouldn't live anywhere else. Notwithstanding time and experience, my enthusiasm is even greater now than when I arrived, hot on the trail of Pablo Picasso and Gertrude Stein. It was the city's buzz as the hub of continental Europe, its ineffable elegance, its inspiring architecture, ranging from High Gothic to High Tech, and its sheer style which made up my mind to stay.

It is impossible to improve on what has already been said about my adopted city by others: 'Paris is the only home for an artist' (Nietzsche); 'Each of us has two countries, his own and Paris' (Josephine Baker); 'Paris is a moveable feast' (Ernest Hemingway) or 'When good Americans die, they go there...' (Oscar Wilde).

To help you extract the most from your stay I have devised four full-day and six half-day itineraries, kicking off with a tour of the islands on the River Seine, where Paris first evolved, and the Latin Quarter on the left bank. The itineraries take in all the famous sites but also include some of the more recondite discoveries I have made over the years, thanks to born and bred Parisian friends and my own insatiable appetite for finding new charms. Not least among these are my favourite cafés and restaurants, which I have included at appropriate moments in these personal journeys. In addition, I have devised five day-trips into the surrounding French countryside, to well-known destinations such as Versailles and less visited ones, such as Monet's house and garden in Normandy — and, of course, to Euro Disney. Any friend of Paris is a friend of mine; this book is a way of showing off my home town. — Grace Coston

Contents

HISTORY &

From Mud Huts to Palaces

Long ago, Paris was a simple village of mud huts nestled on an island in the Seine River. At the far reaches of the Roman Empire, the city *Lutetia*, as the Romans called it, was a mere outpost until Julian built a palace for himself in A.D. 358. Barbarians, Parisii boatmen, and Romans fought frequently on the surrounding plain and all left their mark on the developing character of the Parisians.

Attila the Hun was an unwelcome visitor in the 5th century. The legend of St. Geneviève, the patron saint of Paris, was created when she 'saved' the city from his horde. A mere 19-year-old, she assured the citizens that the Huns would spare the city, and when her forecast proved correct, a cult formed around her.

Clovis I brought his Frankish armies to Gaul shortly thereafter and the Merovingian dynasty was underway. He built the Church of the Apostles to honor the remains of St. Geneviève and was buried there himself. Now the Panthéon sits on the hill, the final resting place for distinguished citizens such as Victor Hugo and Rousseau.

The Capetian dynasty, which began in 987 with Hugues Capet, was a period of growth. The city was improved with public fountains, paved streets, and armed police maintained order. Paris was emerging as a major European city.

Trade continued to boom throughout the 12th century. Merchants united in powerful guilds, controlling city finance and administration. King Philippe Auguste built a big covered market (Les Halles), improved the waterfront for trade and erected a great wall around the city, protecting it and giving it an urban identity.

The Church remained strong during the difficult Dark Ages and with prosperity grew stronger. In addition to Notre Dame, smaller churches arose in its Gothic likeness, and old Romanesque edifices were restored and rebuilt.

Already a commercial and ecclesiastical center, Paris also became the center of scholarship in medieval Europe, the first of the great capitals to have a university. A meeting place for scholars and theologians, controversy and debate became part of the city's character, and remain so today. The upstart scholar Abelard was the first to attract students to the Left Bank, where the university would open. Latin, used in lectures and debates, gave the neighborhood the name it now bears, *le quartier latin*, still today the city's student center.

A City Shaped

In the 14th century, local clothmaker Etienne Marcel led a revolt against the Valois regent, forming an alliance with English forces. All through the Hundred Year's War, control of Paris bounced back and forth between English and French forces. When Joan of Arc laid siege to the city in 1429, Parisians sided with the occupying English

and put up stiff resistance. Things only finally settled down when her campaign to put Charles VII on the throne succeeded.

The period of artistic rebirth that followed under François I continued until the religious crisis provoked the St. Bartholomew Massacre. Thousands of Protestants were killed, but Henri, King of the southwestern realm of Navarre, escaped, and soon became Henri IV, one of France's most celebrated kings. Henri is known to have switched his religion from Catholic to Protestant and back at least six times. The most memorable was of course upon his triumphant conquest of Paris. He chose that moment to convert to Catholicism, in order to please the powerful Church fathers of Paris as well as the general population. "Paris," he said, "is well worth a mass."

Thus began the Bourbon monarchy, France's last. The family lavished plenty of money on the city of Paris, trying to keep the unpredictable citizens, the powerful guilds and the Church content. Louis XIV built hospitals and factories, paved new streets and equipped the city with lanterns. Nonetheless, he preferred to move to his luxurious palace at Versailles, where he was in less danger than in the gloomy old Louvre, surrounded as it was by narrow alleys crowded with houses right up to the palace walls.

In the period leading towards the French Revolution, life in Paris took on two distinct forms. On the one hand, wealthy aristocrats and the burgeoning *bourgeoisie* enjoyed sumptuous decadence, carried on intricate social ceremonies and whirled through the restaurants and theaters of Paris. On the bleaker side, most of the population lived in growing misery, while government debts piled up. A bad harvest in 1788 increased the price of bread and revolution fermented.

The storming of the Bastille prison on July 14, 1789, has long been the symbol of the violent Revolution that shook all of France. The center of Revolutionary activities and government, showcase for the notorious guillotine, Paris was, after the Revolution, resolutely installed as the capital of power. "Paris goes her own way," wrote Victor Hugo, "and France, irritated, is forced to follow."

In the Eye of the Beholder

Through the First Empire, the Restoration, and the Second Republic, Paris continued to solidify its position as the center of government, arts, fashion and trade, and was regarded as one of Europe's finest capitals, despite its sordid slums and squalor of the lower classes.

Joan of Arc

Under the Second Empire (1852–1870) Paris was transformed into the modern city of today. Napoléon III worked with Baron Haussmann, the Prefect of Paris, to carry out extensive urban renewal. Train tracks were set out in all directions, water-mains and a sewerage system were installed, great boulevards and avenues systematically laid out. Slums were razed and the poorest of the poor shoved outside the city in the eastern suburbs.

The last great struggle between the Parisian population and the wealthy *bourgeoisie* took place after the fall of the Empire under the Third Republic. Hostile to the notion of Prussian occupation following the defeat of Napoléon's army and the Republic's capitulation, the citizens withstood a long siege. When the popular National Guard was ordered to disarm, the *Commune de Paris* was proclaimed at the Hôtel de Ville.

Arc de Triomphe

From the Montmartre hilltop came the call to arms, as workers and revolutionaries united in the struggle for better representation in government. The bloody repression was carried out not by the Prussians, but by regular French troops. 25,000 *communards* died fighting or were executed. The bitter and tragic *dénouement* is still a sore spot in the Parisian heart, especially in Montmartre, home to many of the revolutionaries and anarchists who led the battle. Many of the traditional songs heard in cabarets there still recall the *Commune de Paris*.

Paris in the 20th Century

The turn of the century is often referred to as *La Belle Epoque*, a period of gaiety and artistic renewal. The Eiffel Tower rose unbelievably high and the Parisian Metro tunneled below the city. Between 1880 and 1940, Paris was home to more artists than any other city in the world, including Picasso, Debussy, Zola, Diaghilev, Piaf.

The city was saved heroically in World War I when General Galliéni rushed troops to a counter-offensive in the Marne River valley using all available means. Every taxi in town was requisitioned to carry soldiers to the front.

During World War II Paris was not so lucky, and suffered German occupation for four dreary years. The city was not destroyed, although charges of dynamite had been placed strategically under monuments. German commander Von Cholitz had orders to blow the city up if the Allies arrived, but he wisely chose to surrender instead.

After the rationing, death and horrors of war, Paris prospered in the 50s and early 60s. Bebop, Rock and Roll and tourists traveled across the Atlantic. In May 1968, the city saw its most important upheaval since the Commune. Opponents to the Algerian War, disenchanted students and trade unions struck together and paralyzed Paris. The great Charles de Gaulle himself fled the city, just as kings and emperors had done before him, fearful of the wrath of its citizens.

In 1977, reform made it possible for Parisians to elect a mayor for the first time. Jacques Chirac has since presided over the City Council at the Hôtel de Ville. In addition, each *arrondissement* elects a mayor, and the administration of many city affairs is delegated out to separate town halls.

Since 1981, the President has been François Mitterrand, elected for two seven-year terms. As President, he has implemented a vast plan of public works in the city. Like Napoléon III, he will certainly leave his signature on the capital. Among the great projects of the past decade: the improvement of the Louvre Museum with the construction of the Pyramid, the Opéra at La Bastille, the new Finance Ministry at Bercy, the Great Arch at La Défense, La Villette Museum and Park, the Arab World Institute, the Orsay Museum, extensive new road and tunnel systems to ease traffic, development of outllying areas, and improved public transportation. Side by side with the works of Philippe Auguste and Baron Haussmann, these achievements create new harmony in the city.

The spirit of the city today is still a mixture of fractious Gaulish rebellion and refined Roman arts, spiced with the exotic contributions of immigrants from Africa and Asia. A mad poet in Montmartre, a fashion model in diamonds at the Dior boutique, an African student on the Left Bank, an early-rising baker kneading *croissants*: Paris is home to all.

Place du Tertre, Montmartre

A FEW MILESTONES

52 B.C.: *Lutetia* is the Roman name for the primitive city occupied by the Parisii.

A.D. 300: Germanic invasions. The city settles on the Ile de la Cité and takes the name of Paris.

451: Paris repels the Huns with the help of St. Geneviève.

6th century: The Frankish people settle in Paris.

987: The Capetian dynasty begins, bringing years of prosperity.

12th century: Trade booms. Notre Dame built. Philippe Auguste orders the construction of a great wall around the city.

13th century: The University of Paris and the Sorbonne created.

1356-58: Revolt led by Marcel.

1527: The St. Bartholomew massacre.

1594: Henri IV takes Paris.

1682: Louis XIV moves into Versailles palace.

1789: The storming and capture of the Bastille prison.

1793: Execution of Louis XVI.

1804-48: The first Empire, under Napoléon Bonaparte, followed by the Restoration of the (constitutional) Monarchy.

1848: Revolution in Paris, the Second Republic declared.

1860: The number of *arrondisements*, or districts, rises from only 12 to 20.

1853-1870: Under the Second Empire, Haussmann gives Paris its present shape and appearance.

1870-1871: Paris under seige by the Prussian Army.

1871: The *Commune de Paris* civil rebellion ends in bloodshed.

1889: World Fair.

1940-44: German Occupation.

May 1968: General strike paralyzes the city.

1977: Elections for mayor of the city are held for the first time, Jacques Chirac has held the post since.

1981: François Mitterand, President of the Republic, initiates a major plan for renewing the city including Le Grand Louvre, the Opéra at Bastille, the Arch of La Défense, etc.

1989: Celebrations in honour of the Bicentennial of the French Revolution, and 100th birthday of the Eiffel Tower.

The Coronation of Napolean I

Day itineraries

Day 1

A City is Born

Begin your first full day in Paris on the spot where the city itself first started. From there, wind your way through the mosaic of peaceful or lively neighborhoods on the celebrated Left Bank, past the Gothic cathedral of Notre Dame and along the banks of the Seine River. Discover the Latin Quarter, a student hang-out since Roman times, with a distinctive mix of university scholarship and all-hours entertainment. The mood changes to a peaceful one in the Luxembourg Gardens, and you can calmly make your way to

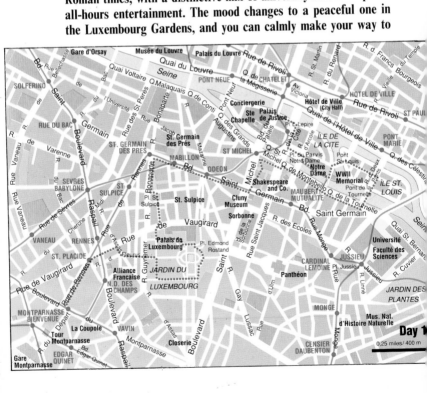

Day 1

0.25 miles / 400 m

Sainte Chapelle

the top of the city's tallest office building, **La Tour Montparnasse**, in time for sunset.

Begin early in the morning and wear your most comfortable shoes. This walking tour takes you from the center of the city towards its southern end, with plenty of places to stop and rest your feet. So travel at your leisure; you can always hop on the Metro to speed to the next destination.

The Ile de la Cité (Metro: Cité), one of two islands in the Seine, site of the earliest primitive city, and later the Roman administrative center, is the main office of the French police and the Court of Justice, in the **Conciergerie**. The forbidding castle stands on the foundations of the city's first royal dwelling. Later, it held prisoners during the French Revolution, including Queen Marie Antoinette.

In this rough setting is a sparkling diamond, the **Sainte Chapelle**. The Gothic chapel (follow the sign inside the main entrance on the Cour du Mai) was built by Saint Louis, King of France, in 1264. The proliferation of deep-colored glass windows in scalloped stonework and the excellent restoration of the walls and columns inside this narrow, vaulting chapel lend it a delicate beauty. Chamber music lovers should note the bulletin board with concert schedules. The chapel is open daily from 10 a.m., but is sometimes inaccessible when notorious bandits are on trial in the Court next door.

On your way to Notre Dame, take a detour to **Place Lépine**, for

Book stalls on the banks of the Seine

the daily flower and bird market. Flower sellers are there from 9 a.m. to 7 p.m., except Sunday, when birds are the specialty. Walk round the corner to the **Parvis de Notre Dame**, a cobbled terrace in front of the great cathedral.

Notre Dame's stone foundation was laid in 1163 but it was only completed about 200 years later. The scene of medieval justice (executions were carried out here), revolutionary disregard (converted to a "Temple of Reason" and became a sort of wine cellar) and the coronation of an emperor (Napoléon I), the cathedral's ancient walls are steeped in history, reflected in the innumerable faces and figures carved upon them. The three portals to the cathedral are typical examples of gothic religious art, each a "book" for the illiterate of the Middle Ages, recounting the stories of the Bible and the lives of saints. Inside, 29 separate chapels line the nave, transept and choir. The **Rose Windows**, 31 feet (nine meters) in diameter, have been restored but parts of them still date from the 13th century.

The carved wooden choir stalls are early 17th century, and the **Pietà Statue** decorating the large altar at the far end of the cathedral was commissioned by Louis XIII during the same period, an offering in thanks for the birth of his son and heir to the throne, who eventually completed the memorial. In veneration on either side of the fallen Christ and his earthly mother are statues representing the regal father and son.

The **Trésor** (closed on Sunday and religious holidays), also in the rear of the building, is the cathedral's museum, displaying religious artifacts, richly embroidered robes and jeweled chalices.

As you leave the church, you will see signs to the **Bell Tower**, and if you are up to a 270-ft (82 meters) spiraling ascent, you can visit the huge brass bell and come eye-to-eye with the devilish gargoyles which contemplate the city from their privileged perch.

Leave the cathedral, walk around the right through the park to the end of the little island.

Notre Dame

There you will find an unusual and starkly moving monument in memory of World War II deportees (**Monument de la Déportation**) set down into the ground. Descend into the pit through narrow passages between thick, rough walls, and meet the black metal bars. There is a feeling of desolation. Yet at the same time, the monument is strangely calm: a sheltered, windless sun trap inviting rest and reflection.

From there, take the Pont St. Louis to the next island, the placid **Ile St. Louis**.

The attractions on this 'island of calm' in the storm of the city are the shady riverfront, the fashionable art galleries and tea

Notre Dame Interior

rooms, and at 31, Rue St. Louis en l'Ile, **Berthillon**, where you can sample what is often called the best ice cream in Paris.

Back across the River Seine, a walk along the quais gives you a fine view of Notre Dame and its flying buttresses, as well as an oppor-

A legend in St. Germain des Prés

tunity to browse at the characteristic green **bookstalls**, where you also find postcards, prints and maps. There are some collector's items to be ferreted out here, but the casual stroller finds that even if prices aren't different from the bigger bookshops, the ambience makes buying a pleasure.

More books, in English mostly, are in store at the historic **Shakespeare and Co.** on the tiny Square Viviani (Metro: St. Michel). Fans of James Joyce know that Paris was his second home and that owner Sylvia Beach was his banker and publisher of his once-scandalous novel, *Ulysses*. The spirit of famous and would-be expatriate writers haunts the shop, which is well worth exploring.

Now you are smack in the centre of the **Latin Quarter**, one of the busiest parts of town favored by students, shoppers and good-time seekers. These narrow ways, redolent with Greek and Middle Eastern cooking, busy with movie house lines and strolling entertainers, recall much older times, despite the electric lights and modern fashions. Street performers set up here as they have for centuries, and pass a hat among the crowd. Through the occasional kitchen door left ajar you may see a chef in his white apron spooning up steaming heaps of Algerian *couscous*. Big hunks of lamb meat are roasting in the windows of sandwich shops; a long sharp knife cuts the thin slices off into an open loaf of bread. At the miniscule **Théâtre de la Huchette**, the troupe has been playing Ionesco's *The Bald Soprano* for over 50 years.

Amble down the pedestrian streets of La Huchette and La Harpe up to **Boulevard St. Michel**. Walk up to the crossroads at **Boulevard St. Germain**, where the two almost legendary streets meet and set the limits of the famous Latin Quarter.

At the corner, the **Cluny Museum**, the city's only surviving Gothic residence, stands next to the ruins of a Roman bath house, a second-century vestige. This is really one of the best museums in a city boasting some of the world's finest. The building lends itself perfectly to the display of furnishings, fabrics, stained glass, architectural ornaments and religious reliquaries from the Middle Ages. Upstairs, the Cluny's prize is the series of tapestries known as *The Lady and the Unicorn*, a 15th-century marvel depicting the five senses as well as a sixth, mysterious and unexplained one to be left to your imagination.

After much medieval food for thought, you will be thinking of some more terrestrial fare, and you will find plenty of choice up the Blvd. St. Germain at the crossroads called **Odéon** (Metro: Odéon). Our recommendation: the **Chope d'Alsace**, at N° 4, will satisfy the heartiest of appetites with typical food from the east of France (especially *choucroute* – sauerkraut with a selection of pork cuts and sausages), grilled meats and seafood. The list of daily specials, often as long as the regular menu, is based on the chef's mood and the morning's market. Prices (count on about 180 Francs per person) are fair for the quality and quantity served, the wine list is tempting, and the desserts will give you the inspiration needed to make it through to the end of the meal.

Thus revived, your next step is to continue up the boulevard towards **St. Germain des Prés**. Along the way, you pass Rue de Buci on the right and Rue Mabillon on the left, both leading to colorful markets. There are shops for every kind of clothes all along the way, from the classic Marcel Fuks for men to the wacky, unisex Atomic City and the voguish Comme ça des Halles for women on the cusp of fashion.

The church of St. Germain des Prés, (Metro: St. Germain des Prés) though one of the city's oldest (built in the 11th and 12th centuries, Romanesque in style) is not one of the loveliest. The *place* is better known for the cafés **Flore** and **Deux Magots** and the **Brasserie Lipp**,

hangouts for the literati since Jean-Paul Sartre and Simone de Beauvoir held court there.

Turn down rue Bonaparte, away from the church and the traffic, to find another stylish row of shops – even Yves St. Laurent is here, with a shop on the pleasant **Place Saint Sulpice** (Metro: St. Sulpice).

Less animated than St. Germain, this square and its 19th-century fountain have a dignified, restful charm. The church, where author Victor Hugo was married, is welcoming despite its monumental proportions; there

St. Sulpice

is a fine old pipe organ inside (check the bulletin board for scheduled concerts); the first chapel on the right was decorated by Eugène Delacroix, one of the greatest painters of the Romantic period. As you leave the church, look up to the building on the opposite side of the square – you may see actress Catherine Deneuve leaning out of her window!

As afternoon wends its way to evening, just a short walk down Rue Ferou brings you to the **Luxembourg Gardens**. Enter at the gate next to the **Petit Luxembourg Museum**, which shows an ever-changing selection of art exhibits, and reach the central fountain by way of the **Palais du Luxembourg**, once a royal palace and today seat of the French Senate. Look straight over the top of the palace on a clear day and you can see the Sacré-Coeur Basilica on the Montmartre hilltop, like a fat white pigeon roosting above the city.

Take a break in the sunshine under the shade of the chestnut trees.

Quiet corner on Rue Bonaparte

This park is a favorite with many Parisians, because of its elegance and central location. But don't tarry after dark, however tempting, or you'll find yourself camping out for the night behind locked gates, which are closed at nightfall by bell-ringing guardians.

Exit the park onto Rue de Fleurus, where Gertrude Stein and her life-long companion Alice B. Toklas lived and reigned over artistic society and the "Lost Generation" at N°. 27. Their *coterie* included Hemingway, Picasso, Ford Madox Ford, Cézanne, Matisse and other

artists in that period from 1907 to her death in 1946. Although these luminaries are gone from the street now, you might run into Joan Baez, if she happens to be staying in her house there.

Turn right on **Notre Dame des Champs** (Metro: St. Placide) to reach Rue de Rennes and from there you can walk straight

Relaxing in Luxembourg Gardens

down to Montparnasse or take the subway and arrive at the big black tower dominating the skyline.

To get a view over the territory you've covered, take the superfast elevator to the 56th floor terrace and rooftop. At this height, the traffic below is seen but not heard; and wide avenues ribboned in green trees stretch away below the rooftops with their characteristic red chimney pots. The glassed-in bar provides signs with information on what you are seeing from each point of reference. But the helicopter pad on the very top (59 stories high) is more exciting; open to the wind and seemingly unbounded on the sides, there is a slight thrill of danger (but no real danger in fact) – perhaps this is why there are not usually too many people up here!

To see where you've been, look due north and you should spot the green sward of the Luxembourg Gardens, and further in the distance, the two square towers of Notre Dame.

At dusk, the sun sets over the hills beyond the Eiffel Tower. On a good clear evening, we recommend this as the best place to watch the natural fireworks at the end of day, and the sparkles of artificial light blooming one by one across the city landscape. The Tower closes at 10 p.m. from Sunday to Thursday; 11 p.m. on Friday, Saturday and before holidays.

Back on the street, you can head for dinner at one of Hemingway's favorites: the **Closerie des Lilas** (171 Blvd. Montparnasse) or **La Coupole** (102 on the same street).

The first has a subdued atmosphere and a piano bar; the second is a gay and noisy place to see and be seen in. Both have plenty of variety on the menu; for a complete meal

La Coupole

with wine, count on at least 200 Francs per person, but you can do it for less. They're open late, as are many of the neighborhood restaurants, cafés and bars, and there are plenty of taxis (though you may have to compete!) to carry you back to your hotel.

Day 2

Victory and Revolution

Today we leave the Middle Ages and the Renaissance behind and begin with a panoramic view of Napoléon's Paris. While erecting monuments to his victorious foreign campaigns, he, and Baron Haussmann, created the shape of Paris as we now know it. See how the city has remained the same, yet continued changing, as you venture from Napoléon's star through royal gardens to the redeveloped Les Halles and the Georges Pompidou Center, traveling over two centuries along the way.

The first half of this day is spent walking the long straight line known as the **Triumphal Way**. A major aspect of Parisian geography, it is not very intimate, and perhaps no longer the most spectacular. Yet the Champs Elysées is still famous. A hint for those with tired feet: ride down the avenue in a green Parisian bus (N°. 73) and save some energy for later.

The **Arc de Triomphe** (Metro: Charles de Gaulle-

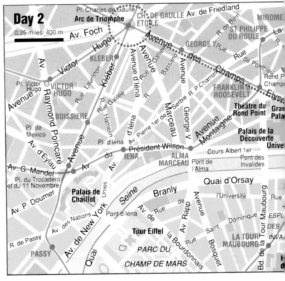

Etoile) is a familiar monument straddling a hectic traffic circle. Construction began in 1806, but it wasn't completed until 30 years later, all in commemoration of the victories of Napoléon Bonaparte's armies. In 1920, the arch became the marker for the **Tomb of the Unknown Soldier**; a Flame of Remembrance was lit, and became a site for veterans' ceremonies and homages by visiting dignitaries.

Arc de Triomphe

It was 'the other Napoléon' (nephew of the Corsican original, known to some as 'Napoléon the Little') who ordered the city planning that gave the **Place de l'Etoile** its name of 'star'. With the Prefect of Paris, Baron Haussmann, he gave Paris its wide boulevards flanked by chestnut trees, including the 12 avenues that radiate out from the Arc de Triomphe. Partly motivated by the need to control rebellious crowds (hence the wide, straight thoroughfares), the two of them created an architectural legend, and greatly advanced the art of urban planning.

Enjoying the view, you can look over a good part of their creation, which is still in place, including the spacious **Bois de Boulogne** forest to the west and of course the **Avenue des Champs Elysées**.

One hundred years ago, this glitzy strip was little more than a bridlepath. Since then its fortunes have gone up and down. Located near the park, it was once a place for closed carriage rides and intimate suppers in discreet restaurants. Luxurious private homes

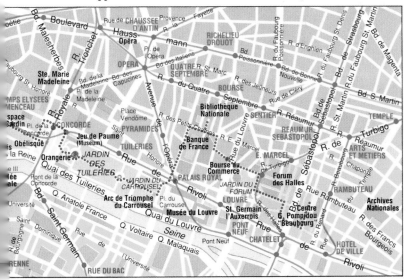

later gave way to sumptuous hotels, expensive shops and desirable corporate addresses. Now, the avenue sparkles at night, but not with the diamonds and bright personalities of its heyday; heavy traffic and neon lights are its rhinestones and jewels.

Movie houses, cafés and fast food places provide most of the entertainment today; the shops and restaurants are generally over-priced; and the folks walking up and down the avenue are mostly kids from the suburbs who come in for hamburgers and a movie.

There are notable exceptions of course, such as the fine **Hotel George V** (on the avenue of the same name, Metro: George V), beautifully decorated, with a fine restaurant and garden terrace. The restaurant **Lasserre** is also nearby (Avenue Franklin Roosevelt, Metro: Franklin Roosevelt), and it is certainly on the list of the top ten in town – for both cuisine and price! Count on 700 Francs per person, but the choice of wine from the outstanding cellar may make that substantially higher. Reservations are necessary at both.

Hotel George V

Despite the fading reputation, it is still fun to stroll down the wide sidewalks along the Champs Elysées and look at people. The sheer size of the street is empha-sized even more by some of the stores such as the **Hippo Citroën** or the **Pub Renault**, where you can check out the latest car models over a thick steak or a beer, and the **Virgin Megastore**, a truly mega book and record shop. At both ends of the avenue, you will find **Le Drugstore**, which has outlived its fashiona-bleness, but still draws a crowd to its American-style restaurant, press stand, and "geegaw" de-partment.

The end of the avenue near Place de la Concorde is far love-lier, with its serene fountains, shady parks and a pair of de-lightful theaters. The **Théâtre Renaud-Barrault** was created by two of France's finest actors, who also happen to be living one of the longest-running love stories ever. You can walk in for a look at the fun décor, or stop for a drink in the bar. The **Espace Cardin** is another prestigious performance space, where a garden restaurant features a buffet lunch. If you're intimidated by eating with celebri-ties, avoid this one!

The **Place de la Concorde**, and its towering, 33-centuries-old

Pub Renault

obelisk from the Temple of Luxor in Egypt, is another city landmark. 85,000 sq yards (70,833 sq m) of cobblestone and traffic cacophony, the place seems just as crowded as it must have been when Louis XVI was beheaded there, and the drivers are almost as aggressive as a crowd at an execution.

Head for the relative peace of the **Jardins des Tuileries**, the long narrow gardens leading to the Louvre. The central alley forms part of the long straight line drawn directly from the Arc de Triomph. Here too, Haussmann went to work tearing down the remains of part of the castle, opening up the streets along the wall. The sunny pools and patches of green lawn alternate with shaded alleys where you'll find an outdoor café, a children's play area, and finally, the **Arc de Triomphe du Carrousel**, a miniature mirror-image of the large arch at the end of the long perspective passing through the two arches and the obelisk. Only in August can you visit the small fair set up for the traditional vacation month and treat yourself to a view from the top of the Ferris Wheel.

Leave the park behind to dash across the busy **Rue de Rivoli** and over to the Place du Palais Royal (Metro: Palais Royal). The adjacent Place Colette is home to the **Comédie Française**, the famous classical theater founded by Molière. Follow the arcades to the entrance of the **Palais Royal Gardens**. About 200 years ago, the Palais really was a royal palace, until Philippe d'Orléans, who was living there, sank

Jardins des Tuileries

deep into debt. He added arcades and rented boutique space to solve his cash-flow problem. The place became a very popular speakers' corner and played an important role in the Revolution.

Today the shops are still there, offering antiques and collector's items, especially coins and military decorations. These dim little boutiques are full of uncommon treasures for those who know how to value them.

Part of the Palais is now occupied by the Ministry of Culture; other apartments are still in private hands. It is said that these apartments are beyond price – families hang on to them forever. It is easy to see why: centrally located yet quiet, soothing to the eye and spirit. Sometimes you can glimpse a high-ceilinged room behind a heavy brocade curtain. Even the children running through the park have something of another era about them, as they roll their hoops along the sandy paths. Within the gardens is a square of black and white columns designed by Burennes, perfectly matched by the window shades of the surrounding buildings.

Slip out the far end of the rectangular gardens; cross over the tiny Rue des Petits Champs. To your left are the **Galerie Vivienne** and the **Galerie Colbert**, recently restored skylit passages with mosaic walkways, leading to Rue Vivienne and the French National Library, not far from the Opéra. To your right, the **Place des Victoires**, a charming circle which was originally built to display the statue of Louis XIV in the center. Now fashion is king, in the young stylists' boutiques **Kenzo** and **Thierry Mugler**. The designers' boutiques are New Age outposts in the regal architecture.

Galerie Colbert

Here you are just around the corner from the restaurant **Pied de Cochon**, one of the best-known in Paris, on Rue Coquillière. As a carry-over from older times, when market deliveries were made in the wee hours before stalls opened up, it is open day and night. One of the favorite dishes of the hard-working market hands was the thick and cheesy onion soup, but you don't have to work hard to enjoy it today. For a complete meal, count on 250 Francs per person.

Modernity is fully upon us in the glinting, high-color complex called **Les Halles**. The name refers to the city food market which clogged up the neighborhood streets from the 12th century until 1969, when it was demolished in the name of safety and urban renewal. Now a more ordinary commerce takes place in about 200 boutiques of every sort and kind inside the multi-level shopping center (Metro: Les Halles).

Walk right around the center by way of Rue Berger and the lively **Place des Innocents**. There is a permanent fashion parade of the wackiest looks here, and a few characters who look like they are trying to hitch a ride to Mars. Those who knew the square before renewal deplore the high-priced boutiques that have replaced all of the good old places, but it must be admitted that it is as animated and attractive as ever. The **Café Costes** is a favorite watering hole and meeting place, with its distinctive black-on-black designer decor.

At the corner of Rue Berger and **Rue St. Denis**, take a good look up and down the latter. This is the beginning of the city's

The Place des Innocents

'red light' street. The hard core is several blocks down to the left, and not very picturesque. At this level, you can find common sex shops, but also plenty of cheap eateries and stores and a few nicer places (**The Front Page**, with American specialities like spare ribs and chilli and an American-style bar).

All the comings and goings in the pedestrian areas, the variety of commerce and night life help the neighborhood of Les Halles to retain something of its former dynamism. Drifters, bargain hunters, local residents and young people mix like a crazy salad.

Amble over the Boulevard Sebastopol and onto Rue des Lombards. As you wander down this narrow street and then along Rue St. Martin, take a look inside **St. Merri**, a pretty medieval church nestled tightly amidst the shops and restaurants. You may hear music floating out, for there are frequent concerts in the church, or you may hear ringing from above – the church bell has been tolling the hours

Inside Beaubourg

since 1331 and is the oldest in town.

Now you are just around the corner from the most visited attraction in the city, the modern museum known affectionately as 'Beaubourg', though the official name is the **Georges Pompidou Arts and Cultural Center** (Metro: Rambuteau).

The museum has become so popular and gained such a reputation in just over ten years that it is almost hard to remember the passionate debate about its 'inside-out' architecture. Comments like, "clashes with the neighborhood", or, "looks like an oil refinery" are rarely overheard – now Beaubourg *is* the neighborhood. Although the furnishings definitely show wear and tear, the price of popularity, what goes on inside is still as exciting as on Day One.

While many Paris museums seem to be staid, whispery places, this one is an exception the minute it comes in sight. Fire-eaters, mimes, musicians and an assorted crew of urban nomads have adopted the sloping cobbled terrace. Students love the library and music room. The ride is free on the escalators that snake up the outside of the building in a transparent tube to the fifth-floor rooftop cafeteria and viewing platform. To the right of the building is a quartz clock counting the seconds to the year 2000. And further right, between Beaubourg and the St. Merri church, is a colorful fountain of grotesque creatures mixed with modern inventions spouting water in different directions.

The permanent collection is the **National Museum of Modern Art**, on the fourth floor. There is a more serious art-appreciation atmosphere in these well-lit and comfortable rooms. Paintings and sculptures are all modern, and include works from different periods and schools: Fauvism, Cubism, Futurism and various artists including Matisse, Kandinsky, Mondrian, Dubuffet. You can even visit the reconstructed studio of the late Romanian sculptor Constantine Brancusi, on the ground floor level.

These permanent exhibits are

Georges Pompidou Arts and Cultural Center (Beaubourg)

well worth the visit, and generally not too crowded. If you see a long line, it is probably for a temporary show, which Parisians rush to be among the first to visit. Occasionally, they are quite controversial, and you may hear art lovers arguing bitterly on the way out.

On the mezzanine level there is usually a free exhibit, often something zany put up by the **Industrial Creation Center**. It could be a collection of decades of household lamp design, "sonic environments" to immerse oneself in, or an exhibit on mud and clay architecture, to name just a few past offerings.

The **Salle Garance** is for zealous cinephiles, specializing in films that don't often make it to your local movie house. For avant garde sounds, there is the **IRCAM**, a prestigious center for musical research directed by Pierre Boulez. The museum also welcomes dance and theater troupes to its basement stage.

There is a complete posting of all the events and exhibits at

Bouchons, for French cuisine

Beaubourg on the ground floor; some things are free and others not. The information booths stocks brochures in many languages to help you find your way around. There is a very good book and card shop in the museum, and recently a new museum shop has opened, selling modern designer products. Like all national museums, Beaubourg is closed on Tuesday. Unlike others, it stays open until 10 p.m., good news on long summer days!

Dining opportunities abound in this neighborhood. Our suggestions: first, **Bouchons** on Rue des Halles. Here you'll find an elegant atmosphere and good service for the French cuisine, some of it distinctly *nouvelle* (about 200 Francs per person). Downstairs there's a piano bar with a more relaxed tone.

Selection number two is less chic but just as French, **Le Chien Qui Fume** (yes, that does mean "the smoking dog"!), on Rue du Pont Neuf. Hearty French cooking at reasonable prices, as well as all-day service from noon until 2 a.m., have made this dog's reputation (set menus at 160 Francs, including wine).

"The Smoking Dog"

Day 3

A History of Change

This itinerary takes you through one of the most distinctive and well-loved neighborhoods of Paris: the Marais. The beauty of the fine buildings lining the narrow, twisted streets can be traced to the 16th and 17th centuries, when well-to-do Parisians built their hôtels particuliers (private residences) here. Now the Jewish community makes it lively in a very different way. Despite encroaching renewal from Les Halles and Beaubourg, the Marais has managed to remain inviting and unique, a pleasant place to stroll or enjoy a quiet meal.

Past the site of the infamous Bastille prison, marking the limits of the quarter, another transformation is underway: a pleasure boat marina, a shiny new Opera House, and rampant chic spreading up the Rue de la Roquette. Although some grumble that rents are up and artists out, the neighborhood has become the favored address for the hippest art galleries. Several museums are included, and obviously the time spent in them will slow your progression. To complete the whole itinerary in a day, choose one or two museums, and content yourself with the windows of most galleries.

Begin your day at the **Hôtel de Ville** (Metro: Hôtel de Ville). This

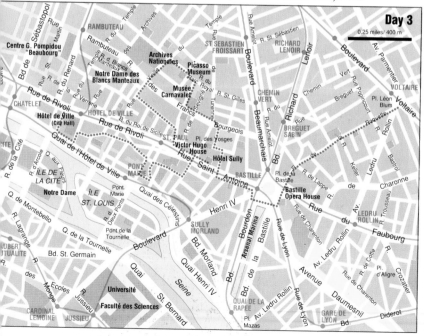

Detail of the Hôtel de Ville

is the main branch of the City Hall, and has been the fiefdom of politician Jacques Chirac since 1977, the only mayor the city has known. One of his reforms was to clean up his glorious office building.

The first Hôtel de Ville was built along the bank of the Seine River during the Renaissance, at the height of the neighborhood's popularity. It was burned to the ground during the insurrection of the Commune in 1871.

Viollet-le-Duc undertook its reconstruction. The Parisian architect is renowned in France for his restoration and re-creation of medieval edifices. Besides the City Hall, he restored Notre Dame and other cathedrals, the castle at Pierrefonds (see *Pick and Choose* section), and the entire city of Carcassone in the south.

There is a convenient post office in the building, and on the Rue de Rivoli there is a new visitors' center. The center is aimed more at residents than visitors, but it is nonetheless worth poking your head in to pick up some of the free literature — including booklets on city museums, concert and festival schedules, and practical information.

You may be tempted to tarry on **Rue de Rivoli**. This is a very busy shopping street, with giants like the **BHV** and the **Samaritaine** department stores, and other specialty shops selling shoes, clothes, candy, whatever. The street leads right up past the Louvre to the Place de la Concorde and is one of the main arteries of Paris.

Hôtel de Ville

But to discover the Marais, you must take quieter paths, and we suggest you begin at the **Saint Gervais Church**. The flamboyant Gothic style of this building is original, not reconstructed. Restoration has been carried out, however, and notably after a German shell exploded here in 1918, killing 51 people at a Holy Friday mass.

Continue up Rue François Miron, contemplating the row of houses from N°. 2 to 14 built in 1732. Farther along, N°. 68 is another remarkable residence, the **Hôtel de Beauvais**, dating from 1665.

Louis XIV gave it to his mistress, and when she was gone, Mozart lived there briefly.

Turn into Rue du Jouy. Walk through the entrance to the **Bibliothèque Forney**. Before it became the city's historical and fine arts library, this building was only known as the **Hôtel de Sens**, which the Archbishop of

Hôtel de Sully

Sens began building in 1470. The pointed towers on the corners are a familiar landmark to Parisians. Later, the mansion was inhabited by Marguerite de Valois, first wife of Henri IV, notorious for her penchant for young lovers.

Walk down Rue Charlemagne to **Rue St. Paul** (Metro: St. Paul). This little street is a favorite, with its antique shops and restaurants. Take it up to Rue Saint Antoine. This wide avenue leads back into the Rue de Rivoli. Cross it and turn right to reach the **Hôtel de Sully**, which now opens its doors to the public as the *Caisse National des Monuments Historiques*. This stellar organization is responsible for organizing the best guided tours of Parisian monuments, museums and sites. Inside, you can visit the lovely gardens and the current exhibit, and also pick up an illustrated map of the Marais (open daily from 10 a.m. to 6 p.m.).

Now turn back down Rue St. Antoine, take a right on Rue Mahler and from there go down the **Rue des Rosiers**. This is the heart of the Jewish Quarter, as one look at the specialized shops and restaurants will tell you. One of the street's best places to eat in **Jo Goldenberg's**. The Goldenberg family is of Russian origin, and their recipes reflect it. Borscht is a favorite starter here, and the stuffed carp is the star of the menu. Prices are moderate, about 180 Francs per person, but if you go for the caviar it will cost more!

Another choice would be to eat your way down the street, stopping at stands for falafel and various sandwiches on pita or rye bread, pickled lemons, smoked sausages and pastries; a mixture of culinary traditions from

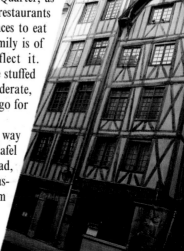

Rue François Miron

The Picasso Museum

both Eastern Europe and the Middle East.

At the end of the street, turn right on Rue Vieille du Temple and follow it up to Rue de la Perle. Make another right to reach the Place Thorigny and the **Picasso Museum**.

The museum is in the **Hôtel Salé**, so-called because its 17th-century owner grew rich through the lucrative activity of collecting taxes on salt. Oddly enough, the very modern masterpieces fit into the well-restored decor superbly. The chandeliers, benches and chairs were designed by Picasso's friend Alberto Giacometti.

The paintings and other works were part of the artist's legacy, and are arranged chronologically. There are also a number of works by other artists which were part of his own collection. The museum opened in 1985, and long lines have been its fate ever since. Even with the crowds, it is worth going in to see so many of this prolific painter's works in one place. It is open from 9.15 a.m. to 5.15 p.m. (10 p.m. on Wednesday) and closed on Tuesday.

Continue your walk down Rue Payenne and past the two pretty little parks bordering it. This part of the Marais has grown more *chic* since the museum opened, and you can spot a number of trendy boutiques and art galleries. Some of them have set up in butcher's or baker's premises, and kept the original shop fronts. Several other Renaissance *hôtels* are currently in the middle of restoration.

Stop on the corner of Rue des Francs Bourgeois at **Marais Plus**, a wonderful bookshop and tearoom. They have many unusual cards, books and gifts, and a great collection of the most eccentric teapots (plus a book about them). Refresh yourself with a big piece of freshly baked cake or pie and a pot of fragrant tea in the simple tearoom. This must be the friendliest, most congenial bookshop in town.

Just around the corner, on Rue Sévigné is the **Carnavalet Museum**. This mansion has also been well-restored and is now the

Hôtel Salé

city's historical museum. Rarely crowded, the exhibits cover aspects of urban life from the Middle Ages through the French Revolution, and also display some of the furnishings and souvenirs of Mme de Sévigné, a 17th-century character known for her voluminous correspondence and virulent gossip. A creaky old place with a quiet little garden, it is open every day (except Tuesday) from 10 a.m. to 6.40 p.m.

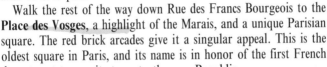

Place des Vosges

Walk the rest of the way down Rue des Francs Bourgeois to the **Place des Vosges**, a highlight of the Marais, and a unique Parisian square. The red brick arcades give it a singular appeal. This is the oldest square in Paris, and its name is in honor of the first French department to pay its taxes to the new Republic.

Victor Hugo's House is open to the public at N°. 6. The author of *Les Misérables* was handy with a carpenter's tools: some of the furniture is crafted by his own hands. It is open from 10 a.m. to 5.40 p.m. (closed Monday). The covered walkways are animated much as they must have been in Hugo's time, with street singers and caliope players. Peek in the shop **Mythes et Légendes**, selling antiques, tapestries and oddments from around the world.

Leave the Marais, down Rue Birague and Rue St. Antoine and go to the **Place de la Bastille** (Metro: Bastille).

In the center of the former site of the notorious prison captured on July 14, 1789, stands the **July Column**. It was erected in the last century to honor the victims of the revolutions of 1830 and 1848. Caught in mid-flight high atop is a golden statue, the *Génie de la Bastille*, a representation of Liberty.

A new fortress has just taken shape here, all silver and glass looking very sleek and impenetrable. It is the **Opéra de la Bastille**, one of President François Mitterand's great projects. Plagued by controversy from the start, and with a multitude of changes in design and administration, the Opéra is still in its infancy. Time will tell if it achieves its goal of making lyric music more accessible to the population of Paris.

Your destination now is **Rue de la Roquette**, branching off near the Opéra and heading east all the way to the Père Lachaise cemetery (*see* itinerary on p.57). Once the women's prison where public executions were spectator sports, the street has shed its grisly reputation and is now a chic and funky place to hang out. A few good old places from the bad old days remain, but they are quickly being replaced by more upscale boutiques and *restos*, French slang for restaurants.

For an indelible souvenir, stop off at the **Tattoo Parlor** at N°. 40. They've managed to stay in business despite their new neighbors selling fancy clothes. If you're ready for dinner, there is some unusual fare and a relaxed atmosphere next door in **Goûts et Couleurs du Monde**, at moderate prices (about 150 Francs).

Further along, at N°. 65, another carry-over is the **Stamp and Coin Shop**, and nearby, a **Model Train Shop**, both havens for col-

July Column, Place de la Bastille

lectors. Otherwise, there are several new clothing shops with some original and exotic items in the windows. Some stylish decorative arts are available in boutiques which specialize in the kinky 50s look.

The main draw here is still the art galleries. At N°. 57, take a look at **J. et J. Donguy**, where two brothers show up-and-coming artists.

Then turn down Rue Keller. There you can visit **Galerie Est, Antoine Candau**, and **Keller**. Take a walk around the corner at Rue de Charonne, past **Clara Scremini**, and up the passageway at N°. 37 to **Leif Stâhle**, run by the Swedish director of the Art Fair of Stockholm.

Lavignes Bastille is one of the best-known in the neighborhood, three-stories high. Andy Warhol has exhibited here.

Take a trip down the Passage Thiéré, where new places are sprouting up, including **Brasil InterArt**, which also sponsors musical evenings. There is even a tiny shop selling hand-crafted American decorative objects called **Tumbleweed**, which might be just the thing if you are an American in Paris who wants to buy a gift for a French friend.

The last street on our agenda is Rue de Lappe. There are more

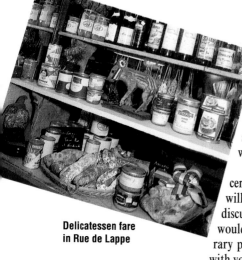
Delicatessen fare in Rue de Lappe

galleries here, including **Galerie la Bastille** and **Claire Burus**. Of course, exhibits in all of the galleries change regularly, so it is impossible to predict exactly what you will find.

Prices may be negotiable; certainly any of the galleries will be glad to inform you and discuss any artist's work. If you would like to take a contemporary painting or sculpture home with you, this is the place to look.

Rue de Lappe is a good place to stop for dinner and have some fun, too. Try eating at **La Galoche**. The name comes from the word for "shoe" used in the region of Auvergne. It was outsiders from that province of France who first settled into the neighborhood, and there are still signs of their influence in the specialty groceries and the faded signs hanging above the shops. La Galoche serves typical hearty fare from the region (150 - 200 Francs) in a warm friendly atmosphere. You can even purchase a pair of the wooden shoes.

Such shoes, however, are not recommended for a night of dancing at the **Balajo**. This fun club is authentic and inexpensive, with its Art Deco look and big dance floor. It is one of the few night spots open on Monday, which is accordion night. Rumba, salsa, java and old rock and roll set the beat. Parisians love to come back here again and again. The crowd gets a bit rowdy at times, but the local renewal has tamed the ambience. In the Balajo, you know you are in Paris, for there is nothing anonymous about it.

Metro station Bastille

Perhaps your day's journey has left you too tired to tango. If so, head for the comfortable seats in the **Brasserie Bofinger** (5-7 Rue de la Bastille), one of the city's finest. Settle back in the old-fashioned decor of brass, mirrors, leather and ceramic. The food is worthy of the setting in the oldest brasserie in town. For 200-250 Francs per person, you can enjoy a real feast; the menu features fresh seafood, *choucroute*, and traditional French dishes and wine.

So, you have an itinerary for a full day of wandering. But whether you stick to these winding streets or drift off onto others, discovery and adventure are in store. This is not the Paris of wide vistas and major monuments, but a series of small surprises, like the Russian dolls for sale on the Rue des Rosiers, packed one inside the other.

To the Eiffel Tower

Today's visit takes place in a part of Paris known by its district number – the 16th – and largely ignored by tourists. It is a luxurious residential neighborhood bordering on the spacious western park of Paris, the Bois de Boulogne. Down by the riverside, the district puts on a much more familiar face at Trocadéro,

Bois de Boulogne

where the monumental **Palais de Chaillot** opens its two wings to frame the city's most famous site: Mr. Eiffel's Tower, over 100 years young and as defiant as ever.

On a map, the **Bois de Boulogne** is a large green rectangle bordered on the far western side by a bend in the Seine River and on the inner side by the 16th district of Paris. The main entrance to the 2,000-acre (872 ha) park is at Porte Dauphine (Metro: Porte Dauphine). Start off early and walk along the Route de Suresne, or adventure off the roadway onto the footpaths, leading to the **Lac Inferieur**, a long and narrow artificial lake.

Share your morning stroll with the Parisians who enjoy the *Bois* as a big back yard. There are always joggers out here, and the lake is popular with rowers. In some parts of the *Bois*, prostitution is practised rather openly by 'hitchhikers' standing near the roadway. In the daytime, of course, it is rarer.

You may see people waiting for the horses to start running at the **Auteuil Race Track**, studying their racing forms and the sports pages. Rose lovers, walk deeper into the park along the Route aux Lacs and the Route de Bagatelle to the **Bagatelle Gardens**. The fragrant park has long been a favorite spot for romance. The expression, *faire la Bagatelle,* has always been a quaint way of saying "make love".

Children, head northward to the **Jardin d'Acclimatation** (Metro: Porte Maillot or Sablons), a must-do attraction for travelers under 10. For a small entrance fee, you and the kids can visit the collection of farm animals, and the kids (sorry, no grown-ups) can climb, roll, swing, slide, run, crawl and jump on a great bunch of toys. For the price of tokens purchased inside, you can board the miniature train, visit a children's museum, go on carousel rides. The *Jardin* has an old-fashioned atmosphere, reinforced by the people who frequent it: wealthy, white-gloved grandmothers from the 16th with tots in navy blue sailor suits, girls in long braids and lace collars.

When you are ready to leave, amble down the footpath known as the *Allée aux Dames.* This leads to the **Fortifications**, an archaeological site revealing the last remains of the old city wall. Walk out by the Route des Lacs where it leads to the Place de la Porte de Passy. Cut straight across the wide Boulevard Suchet and veer left on Avenue Ingres into the **Jardins de Ranelagh** (Metro: Ranelagh).

The trees seem to form a vaulting ceiling, green and airy, above

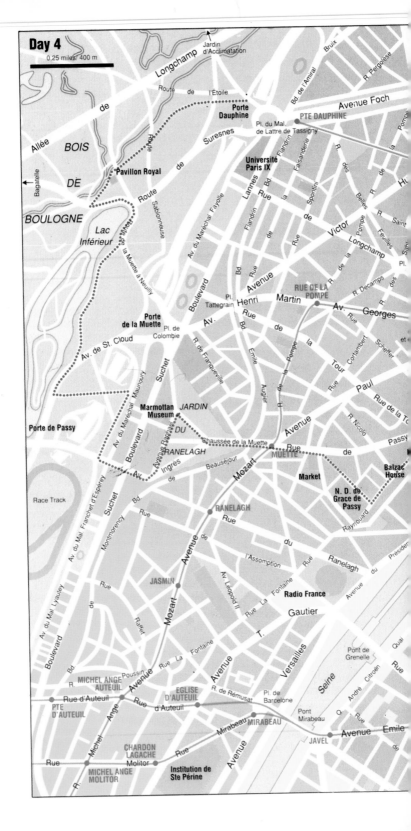

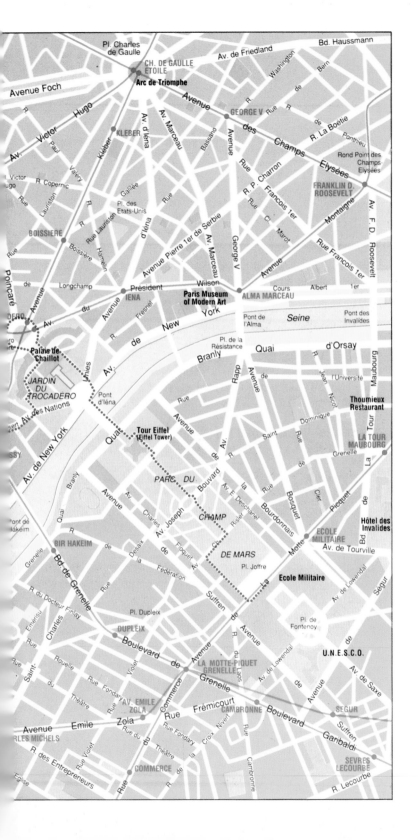

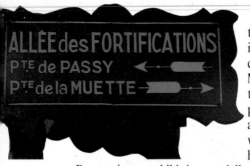

ALLÉE des FORTIFICATIONS
P.TE de PASSY
P.TE de la MUETTE

the soft sandy floor, transforming the sedate little park into a cathedral. This is home to the **Musée Marmottan**, devoted to the work of Impressionist painter Claude Monet. Delicious and colorful as summer itself, works from the last 20 years of his life make up the collection. Downstairs, on exhibit in a specially designed room, are the painter's renowned *Water Lilies*, giant canvases done in his garden in Giverny (see Pick and Choose section). Also on display is the Marmottan family's collection of furniture and medieval manuscripts. Oddly enough, the different types of art seem quite at home together in this lovely old building. The museum opens at 10 a.m., except Monday.

Walk out of the triangular-shaped park by its tip on Avenue de Ranelagh and straight ahead through one of the busiest intersections of the 16th, **La Muette** (Metro: La Muette).

A funny story about this wealthy, rather snobbish part of town: when first incorporated into the city, the area was designated district number 13. Well-to-do residents didn't appreciate the unlucky number, and they used their collective political clout to have it changed. Still today, the very buildings evoke privilege, with their massive wooden doors, decorative carved facades — the architect's name is often engraved by the doorway — and manicured flower beds. *Au pair* girls guide small children across the street; maids carry shopping baskets, *Madame's* list in hand.

Around **Place de Passy** the shopping is made busier than ever by the covered market. Here elegant ladies look over the roast beefs, pinch avocados, sniff the fresh fruits and flowers as they plan their dinner parties. Teenagers turned out in the latest fashions stop for sweets in chic little bakeries. Turn right on the street after the market, Rue de l'Annonciation, and follow it down to the Rue Raynouard (Metro: Passy).

About one block up to the left, you find the **Maison de Balzac**, lending a bit of high-spirited irreverence to the posh neighborhood. The prolific writer lived here from 1840 – 1847, while revising the 90 volumes of his novel series *La Comédie Humaine*. Downstairs, the complex genealogy of the 2,000-odd characters has been mapped out, and Balzac's corrections appear in the margins of original manuscripts. One look at his cramped writing and the extensive annotations and you understand why typesetters charged double to do his books!

Balzac, whose burly profile and strong presence are so aptly captured in the Rodin statue (*see*

Statue of Balzac

A.M. Itinerary No.1), liked to work from 2 a.m. to 5 p.m. One way he kept going was by drinking gallons of black coffee which he concocted himself. That explains the prominent coffee pot. As for the tiny finger puppets also found near his writing table, just imagine the irrepressible author playing out the scenes from his books with them!

Maison de Balzac

Place du Trocadéro

Another feature of Balzac's house is the secret exit leading out to a back street. Without a secretary or an answering machine, he had a way of escaping unwelcome callers. When he wasn't drinking coffee, the author was not averse to spirits, so it seems fitting that the underground passage from his house ends up in what is now the **Musée du Vin** (Wine Museum), located on Charles Dickens square.

This simple little museum is very aptly situated, for the cellar cut into the riverbank hillside that once belonged to the monks of Passy, who made their own wine and stored it there 400 years ago. In the 17th century, the street was crowded with people coming to drink the mineral water flowing from the ground, reputed to have miraculous curative powers. It became a fashionable spot for lovers to meet, and Napoléon himself was seen there frequently.

During the French Revolution, the last monks were chased from the abbey here and the convent destroyed. None of the other build-

ings survived past 1906. The cellars were mostly forgotten until the 60s when the owner of the Eiffel Tower Restaurant started storing his wine there. In 1984, the present museum opened.

The exhibits are a hodge-podge of tools, containers and wax figures; the walls are covered with engravings and drawings relating to wine. The little boutique has a sumptuous selection of vintage wines and all sorts of corkscrews, serving baskets, glasses, decanters, thermometers, books, racks – everything to bring out the oenophile in you. And if it is all too much to resist, you can wind up with a little wine-tasting right on the spot, accompanied by a little snack.

It is a short walk from the Wine Museum to **Place du Trocadéro** at the end of Boulevard Delessert. Follow the garden path up to the **Palais de Chaillot** crowning the hilltop. In the center of the park, steps and ramps to the main alley and big fountains are alive with kids on skates and skateboards, performing intricate manoeuvres in time to their Walkmans.

The outdoor restaurant on the left is called the **Totem**, you get in by taking the entrance to the Musée de l'Homme. The view over the gardens and across the river to the Eiffel Tower is enough to draw you in. The food is also worthwhile, definitely a cut above the usual museum cafeterias. At about 150 Francs per person, it is one of the better deals in the neighborhood.

Steps in the Quartier Trocadéro

The flat terrace between the two wings of Chaillot, lined with golden statuettes, is very busy with African merchants selling bracelets, leather goods and toys to visitors. Beyond, the Trocadéro is a ring of traffic and upscale cafés and bistros.

The curved buildings and monumental landscaping date from the World's Fair of 1937. Now the complex is a formidable bastion of culture. It would be impossible to visit all of the exhibit space in one day, but each of these impressive museums deserves a mention.

The **Musée de l'Homme** is devoted to anthropology. Eskimos, mummies, primitive man, mysterious civilization, all have a place here. One favorite room is the **Salon de Musique**, with a collection of musical instruments through the ages.

The **Musée des Monuments Français** is another favorite. Roman, Gothic and Renaissance architecture and decoration from all over France are represented. A place to wander in dreamily, it is like traveling through the French countryside in a time machine.

A more recent arrival is the **Musée du Cinéma**. Not for the casual visitor, you must take a group tour with a guide, in accordance with the founder's wishes. If you love movies and can understand some French, line up for the one-hour trip through fantasy land. From flip cards and the first still photos, the history of cinema unfolds by way of landmarks like part of the set for Fritz Lang's *Metropolis*, Scarlet's green gown from *Gone With the Wind*, and a severed head from *Psycho*. Tours begin at 10 and 11 a.m.; then at 2, 3 and 4 p.m. The guides are thoroughly familiar with the subject and the exhibits, and if the group is curious, lively and talkative, the tour may go on longer.

Also on the hilltop: the **National Popular Theater** (TNP). It makes you feel as if you have walked into the belly of a whale. The main house seats 1,150; classical works are usually performed. The foyer and the smaller house (Gémier) show less intimidating pieces.

Finally, the **Musée de la Marine**, a maritime museum, makes a special effort for children with many exhibits and activities for them.

All of the above museums are closed on Tuesday.

Now, before your eyes as you cross the Seine River: the Eiffel Tower. The 1,050-foot (320-meter) Tower, once vilified, now reigns as the queen of Parisian monuments. A recent face-lift in time for the Tower's 100th birthday coincided with the expiration of a privately

Ecole Militaire

held lease. The beauty treatment removed tons of rust and a sagging restaurant. New lights paint the metal lattice-work silver and gold at night. The Eiffel Tower is as lovely as a bride, finally, officially wed to the city of Paris after 100 years of turbulent cohabitation.

Be prepared to stand in line in the summer or during a major holiday. The glass-walled elevator jerks up at an alarming angle. The machinery is unique in the world; a special team of employees does nothing but oversee spare parts, which must be made individually.

On the first level, an exhibit and short film recount the story of Gustave Eiffel and the 1889 World's Fair. The Tower was meant to be temporary, no one ever intended that it should become the symbol for Paris. The advent of radio transmission gave the Tower, the world's highest structure when first built, a reason to stay.

History also tells us that the Eiffel Tower was the material for an outrageous scam. A clever con man convinced victims that the Tower was to be torn down and, acting as a discreet government agent, said he was authorized to arrange the sale of the Tower for scrap iron. His first two victims were too embarrassed to expose him; the third was less proud and closer to his cash!

Also on the first level is the restaurant **La Belle France**; always full, so call ahead. Diners certainly come more for the view than the food, which is not outstanding (at about 300 Francs per person).

On the top platform is another restaurant, much better than the first. You reach **The Jules Verne** by a private elevator for patrons only. The dark decor contrasts with the city at your feet, full of color and bright movement. Here too, reserve well in advance to savor the fine *cuisine traditionnelle*. Prices are among the highest in Paris, about 700 Francs per person.

The Tower is open until 11 p.m. weekdays; till midnight on Friday, Saturday and before holidays. Tickets are sold at the base, a different price for each level. The view from each is excellent. The long park stretching away from the riverside and under the Tower's splayed feet is the **Parc du Champs de Mars** (Metro: Bir-Hakeim or Ecole Militaire), once a military drill field. At the far end, is the 18th-century **Ecole Militaire**, France's officer training academy.

A final recommendation, if you haven't been able to dine in the Tower, walk down **Rue St. Dominique**, about half-way down the park. At N° 79, stop in at **Thoumieux,** another sort of Parisian landmark (Metro: ∑Invalides). Open every day, their specialty is the Southwestern *cassoulet*, based on white beans and duck. The waiters in their long white aprons, the happy diners, the din of laughter and cutlery, makes the ambience as appetizing as the food. Informal and inexpensive, dinner costs about 150 Francs per person.

A.M. Itineraries

1. All That's Best of Dark and Bright

This morning you will walk in beauty: from the sublime forms of sculptor Auguste Rodin, to the grand shape of the Napoleonic Empire and on to the arts of high fashion and haute couture. The 7th and 8th districts of Paris, separated by the Seine River, are elegant, distinguished neighborhoods, to put you in a quiet, relaxed mood.

The **Rodin Museum**, at 77 Rue de Varenne opens at 10 a.m. (Metro: Varenne; closed on Monday). In the morning, the rose garden and its still pools are shadowed by the **Hôtel Biron**, built in 1731 as a private residence. Auguste Rodin lived and worked there one hundred years later, and bequeathed it to the State

Map labels:

Morning 1
0,25 miles / 400 m
R. de Ponthieu
Pl. Beauvau
Av. Matignon
Bd. Malesherbes
R. du Faubourg St. Honoré
Rond Point des Champs-Elysées
MADELEINE
R. Royale
Av. Pierre Charron
Rue François 1er
Av. George V
FRANKLIN D. ROOSEVELT
Avenue Montaigne
R. F. D. Roosevelt
des
Av.
CHAMPS ELYSEES CLEMENCEAU
Av. Gabriel
Champs Elysées
Grand Palais
The Scots Kirk
R. J. Goujon
Av. W. Churchill
Petit Palais
Av. E. Tuck
CONCORDE
Place de la Concorde
Obélisque
ALMA MARCEAU
Cours Albert 1er
Cours la Reine
Q. des Tuileries
Pl. de l'Alma
Bateaux Mouches
Pont de l'Alma
Pont des Invalides
Seine
Pont Alexandre III.
Pont de la Concorde
American Church
Pl. de la Résistance
Quai d'Orsay
Air France Terminal
Q. A. France
Rue
Rapp
Avenue
La Tour Maubourg
Rue de l'Université
Mal. Gallieni
Assemblée Nationale
Bd. St. Germain
Saint
Dominique
INVALIDES
Rue
Saint
Dominique
LA TOUR MAUBOURG
Musée de l'Armée (Army Museum)
Hôtel des Invalides
Napoleon's Tomb
St. Louis
Eglise du Dôme
Musée Rodin
VARENNE
Rue
de
Grenelle
de
Varenne
Rue Vaneau
Bosquet
Picquet
de
La Motte
ECOLE MILITAIRE
Av.
de
Av. de Tourville
Pl. Vauban
Pl. Joffre
Av. Duquesne

The Rodin Museum

on the condition that his works be exhibited in the house and park. Though he is now recognized as one of the greatest sculptors of all time, with a technique comparable to that of Michelangelo, Rodin was a figure of controversy in his own time. Some of the early exhibitions of his work brought cries of fraud from 'experts' who claimed that his human figures were so precise they could only have been made by using real bodies to form molds for casting. In this setting, more than any other, the timeless figures do seem to live and breathe, calling out for caresses.

Enter under the gaze of what may be Rodin's most famous statue, *The Thinker*, set up high amid the greenery. To the left, *The Burghers of Calais* reenact the noble gesture that saved their town from the ravages of the English army in the 14th century. Against the wall, *The Gates of Hell* is a monumental work wreathed with demons and the damned.

Cannons at Les Invalides

Inside the house, the wooden floors, marble staircase, gilt mirrors and French windows embrace large works, including the prominently displayed *Adam* and *Eve*, as well as small ones, such as *The Kiss*, a delicate study in white marble. There are works by other artists, including Camille Claudel, Rodin's assistant and mistress. The difficulties of the creative life at the time were multiplied for her as a woman, and she eventually lost her mind and was all but forgotten in a mental institution. Recently, the film *Camille*, starring Isabelle Adjani and Gerard Depardieu, created renewed interest in the artist and her relationship with the great master.

Out the back door, you can wander under the grape arbor and rest on a sunny bench in this remarkable place: so full of peace and so fraught with turbulent feeling.

When you leave the museum, turn left onto Boulevard des Invalides and walk to **Place Vauban**. Here you have a fine architectural vista offered by the Avenue de Breteuil, stretching out like a green carpet in one direction, and the giant complex known as **Les Invalides** on the other.

The first building that stands out is the golden-domed **Church of St. Louis**, completely regilded as part of the city's bicentennial facelift in 1989. Therein lies the **Tomb of Napoléon I**, six layers of coffins beneath a sarcophagus of dark red stone. He is kept company by a number of great generals and his son, the ill-fated 'King of Rome'. The decoration inside the church is distinctly military: flags captured from enemies of the Empire are hung on the walls.

The other vast wings of the Invalides were initially built as a veterans' home, but today's old soldiers make do with more commonplace housing, while the buildings house the **Army Museum** and administrative offices.

The museum is the world's largest of its kind, and exhibits cover everything from suits of armor to the taxi cabs mobilized

Pont Alexandre III

for the Marne offensive in WWI. In the summer months, a nightly sound and light show brings back the glory (check the announcements out front for times and languages).

Napoleonic images of grandeur are projected beyond the main entrance across the windswept **Esplanade des Invalides**. Both sides of the streets lead away to many government Ministries, Embassies and official residences. The *ensemble* culminates in the **Pont Alexandre III**, perhaps Paris's most splendid bridge (Metro: Invalides). Built

in 1900, the bridge spans the Seine River with a single metal arc. The golden statues and distinctive lamp posts are unmistakably representative of Paris itself.

Crossing the river, you arrive right in the middle of the **Grand Palais and the Petit Palais**. Both are museums with permanent and changing exhibits (both closed Tuesday). Look at the big posters outside to find out what's on. Occasional blockbuster shows bring

Avenue Montaigne

crowds that form into a long line wrapped all the way around the park. The typical turn-of-the-century wrought-iron and glass 'crystal palaces' were built for the 1990 World Fair. The gardens around them are pleasant and shady; take a breather and people-watch (Metro: Franklin Roosevelt or Champs-Elysées Clemenceau).

You'll need your breath for exclamations on the last leg of this itinerary: the main branch of 'The Golden Triangle' of shopping streets: **Avenue Montaigne**. Here you can gaze at the displays set up for **Chanel**, **Cartier**, **Dior**, **Vuitton**, **Nina Ricci**, **Ungaro**, **Valentino** ... and more than your combined credit cards could imagine. Even if you don't venture into the boutiques, you can get an eyeful just strolling down the street, which is of course kept spotlessly clean and often decorated in holiday style by the high-tone tenants.

This brings you back to the riverbank at **Alma Marceau** (Metro: Pont d'Alma), where you can stop in a café or brasserie for lunch, or head for a **Bateau Mouche Tour Boat** just underneath the bridge. You can pick up a snack as you wait for the departure, and spend a pleasant hour off your feet, gliding by the scenery. Boats leave every 20 minutes or so in summertime; tickets are 30 Francs for adults, 15 for kids under 14. Don't bother trying to listen to the static and crackle of the multi-lingual, taped commentary, just sit back and look. Sure, it's 'touristy', but even nonchalant Parisians enjoy the unique view from the water.

2. Paris is a Village

This suggestion for a peaceful morning in eastern Paris brings a hint of mystery, a touch of the exotic, and a lunchtime 'find'.

Those who know it love to return, and some who go there never leave–such as Frédéric Chopin, Molière, Rossini, and more recent luminaries including Edith Piaf, Gertrude Stein, Oscar Wilde and Jim Morrison. The place, of course, is the Père Lachaise Cemetery, in eastern Paris, the city's largest and loveliest burial grounds (Metro: Père Lachaise).

At the main entrance on Boulevard de Ménilmontant, visitors can pick up a map with the locations of the more famous gravesites, and the small bookstore also sells a surprising variety of guides to Père Lachaise. Indeed, most of the people wandering about seem more curious than bereaved.

At first glance, this older part of the cemetery appears to make use of aboveground burial, but look closely and see that the tiny houses in this city of the dead are actually small chapels, often in disrepair. Walk up Avenue Principale and turn right to find the monument marking the grave of Heloïse and Abelard. She was a student of the controversial theologian in the 12th century, and secretly became his wife. Her father's fury separated them, he in a monastery and she in a convent, but they left their letters to posterity, professing a pure and faithful love untrammelled by circumstance.

Make your way along the shady paths to the chapel on the hilltop for a view over the stalwart chestnut trees, spreading like guardian spirits over the myriad monuments. You may see the benches occupied by old women feeding the many cats who make their home here.

Others come to visit the grave of Allan Kardec, spiritist, and leave odd mementos or practice bizarre rites in front of the bust marking his tomb. Of greater historic interest is the Mur des Fédérés, where the last of the rebels of the Paris Commune stood up to regular troops in 1871. The bullet holes are still visible in the wall against

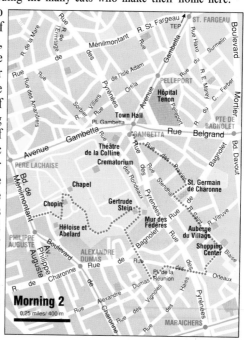

Morning 2
0.25 miles/ 400 m

Chopin's tombstone, Père Lachaise Cemetery

which the anarchists were lined up and shot. A bit farther on along the wall is the Jardin du Souvenir, with many monuments to the dead of World War II. Some of the works in memory of those who died in Nazi concentration camps are frightening reminders of that horror, dedicated to the victims of Auschwitz, Ravensbruck, Buchenwald and others. There are also monuments to different members of the French Resistance. If you are especially interested in this period, you may be able to meet veterans or historians here, deep in *souvenir*, the French word for 'memory'.

Leave the quiet behind slowly, exiting onto Rue de la Réunion (named for the Indian Ocean island which is a French territory), a street more likely to be jammed with baby-strollers than cars. This is the sort of neighborhood where people close up the shop and go home for lunch, with a *baguette* of bread under the arm.

Place de la Réunion looks as if it had been picked up and transported from some much smaller town in France, or even directly from the tropics, as the local African community adds a colorful dimension to the tiny circle and park. A busy market (Thursday and Sunday until 1 p.m.) is a good place to mingle with the neighborhood crowd – see how different they are from the shoppers in the 16th (Day 4 Itinerary) or on Avenue Montaigne. (A.M. Itinerary1).

Rue St. Blaise

Continue through this neighborhood of small shops and furniture craftsmen down the Rue des Orteaux and under the old train line to rue des Clos. This takes you to Le Village St. Blaise, tucked discreetly into this eastern end of Paris (Metro: Porte de Montreuil). Part of the neighborhood is a modern public housing development and shopping center done up in a purple color scheme, animated by residents who obviously enjoy the different squares and pedestrian zones created by the architects. The quality and originality of the architecture and planning belie the 'moderate rent' nature of the housing and business complex.

Up the street, the older buildings that remain have found new life. Most notably, a little restaurant called the Auberge du Village (Place des Grès, closed Sunday), pops out of the landscape as if from a child's cardboard picture book. But in fact, it is all quite real: the cobbled terrace, the low ceilings, the flowerpots in the windows, and the good French food and wine. The prices are moderate (the works for under 250 Francs, set menus start around 80 Francs), the clientele is local business people and employees.

Another find is an Algerian restaurant called **Le Village de Paris** (24 Rue St. Blaise). *Couscous*, the main item on the menu, is very popular in Paris, and not only with the large North African population. This family restaurant is warm and homey.

Big dishes are brought out to the table and you garnish your plate as you choose with a selection of exotic appetizers. Then follows the *couscous:* four varieties of fluffy semolina, a bowl of piping hot vegetables and sauce; a little tub of hot pepper sauce for spice; and a choice of mutton, chicken or beef.

After the meal, pass around the plate of fresh dates. The charming waiters offer flowers to women diners as they leave. If you like Algerian food, head directly here, you can't find better, and you can't beat the prices (150-200 Francs gets you any dish on the menu).

St. Germain de Charonne

There are other nice places on the street that you'll be tempted to 'discover' yourself, and even a cute tea room for delicate eaters (**Le Damier**).

Watching over rue St. Blaise, its single rose window like a benevolent eye, is **St. Germain de Charonne**, whose country-church character suits the neighborhood well. This church is so popular for weddings that Parisians sign up a year in advance for the pleasure of saying *oui* at the altar and having their wedding pictures taken out front.

Walk up the steps next to it. Turn right

on the narrow **Chemin du Parc de Charonne** bordering the churchyard and cemetery for a glimpse of Paris as it was a century ago. A few modern apartment buildings have begun to make an appearance here, but the street and neighborhood are still home to small manufacturers and workshops for craftsmen.

This is a quiet and simple part of Paris, where older residents lean out the windows to chat, and children skip home from school, wearing their schoolbags on their backs. In the face of skyrocketing rental fees and luxury building booms, this eastern pocket remains a place where ordinary Parisians can live and enjoy themselves as citizens of the city. Take a good look now before real estate speculation forever changes the face of the 20th district.

The Rue des Prairies and Rue des Pyrénées will take you back to the **Place Gambetta** (Metro: Gambetta), the heart of the 20th arrondissment. The Town Hall, police station and a big hospital are here along with cafés, restaurants, subway and bus stations, a movie theater and the nearby Théâtre de l'Est Parisien (TEP) at 159 Avenue Gambetta and the national Théâtre de la Colline at 15 Rue Malte-Brun.

Both have on their programs a good variety of contemporary French plays (though not exclusively). So if you are a fan, this is the place to come for French productions that may lack the hoopla of some of the more elegant halls, but are serious and interesting in their pursuit of dramatic art.

Your walk through this district has taken you into intimate Paris, the city that belongs to people who read headlines rather than make them, and to visit some of the city's most famous inhabitants whose influence, even in death, is with us. Far from the bright lights, but close to the heart, here then, is the peaceful village of Paris.

The Opéra

3. Shopping Mania

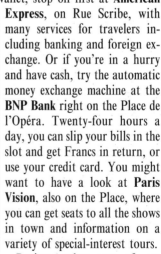

Looking for a special gift? Feeling guilty about leaving the kids behind? Want to wow 'em at the office with fashions straight from Paris? Follow this trail and load up on goodies, or just enjoy a plunge into the busiest shopping district in town. If you're a window shopper only, this can easily be done in a morning, but if you go on a spree, it may take all day!

Get into the flow at the Place de l'Opéra and in the big Parisian department stores, mobbed by locals and tourists, and packed to the rafters with merchandise. Detour by a small but divine shop, and taste the wares upstairs. Wind up in the most exclusive shopping site of all – and don't forget to count your change!

There's one metro station in Paris that everyone seems to pass through regularly, and it bears the name of the famous building above it, **The Opéra**. It's a lively neighborhood, the hub of the **Grands Boulevards**, and business center to banks, travel companies, and the nearby Stock Exchange (*La Bourse*).

If you need to replenish your wallet, stop off first at **American Express**, on Rue Scribe, with many services for travelers including banking and foreign exchange. Or if you're in a hurry and have cash, try the automatic money exchange machine at the **BNP Bank** right on the Place de l'Opéra. Twenty-four hours a day, you can slip your bills in the slot and get Francs in return, or use your credit card. You might want to have a look at **Paris Vision**, also on the Place, where you can get seats to all the shows in town and information on a variety of special-interest tours.

Business taken care of, get down to fun. Start at the **Palais Garnier**, as the Opéra building is officially known. The 'wedding cake' was completed in 1875, the crowning achievement of the plan designed by Haussmann to open up the center of Paris.

You can walk into the vaulting foyer for a glimpse at the eclectic decor, and on days when no rehearsal is in progress, you can go into the theater itself. A splendid surprise awaits you in the heavens: painter **Marc Chagall's ceiling**, a frolicsome work in blue and pearl tones, in striking contrast to the overall sombre red and gold opulence of the hall.

Just across the street is the **Grand Hotel**, and its sidewalk café, the **Café de la Paix**. This is a prime spot for indulging in the art of seeing and being seen, or setting a *rendezvous*. The expansive (and expensive!) café, taking up a whole corner of the Place de l'Opéra, is not the place to go when you're in a hurry, but, as the name suggests, a place for a moment of peace in the midst of the crowd. If you really need to get out of the fray, there's a cozy bar tucked away on the far side of the main hall of the hotel. The bartenders there have invented a few special cocktails that you won't fast forget.

Marc Chagall's ceiling

Revived, refreshed, and pockets lined with French money, head for **Les Grands Magasins**. These department stores sprang up in Paris in the last century and have been popular ever since. On Boulevard Haussmann you'll find the **Galeries Lafayette** first of all. Walk in and orient yourself by heading for the central escalators and the store directory in French and English, plus a bilingual hostess who can help you find that perfect gift for Aunt Ada. Other services at the store include a fashion consultant, currency exchange, and 'duty free' forms for recovering sales taxes at the airport. Fashion is the biggest seller here, whether it's off-the-rack designer or the Galeries' own label. Accessories are fun shopping: stockings, scarves, headwear and other items you never knew you needed before.

Across the street is **Marks and Spencers**, the British chain store, which seems just as popular as its French cousins. And another block down is **Printemps**, which advertises that it is "the most Parisian department store." It certainly is the most beautiful inside: the domed ceiling built in 1923 is now classified as a historic monument. The perfume department has the largest selection in Paris. There are

Printemps

makeup demonstrations and fashion shows scheduled almost every day, and you find the same services for English-speaking tourists as in the Galeries.

The street along the two stores takes up the overflow of commerce and all along fast and furious sales pitches fly for revolutionary cookware, two-for-one deals of a lifetime, the latest development in travel irons. There are plenty of odd-lots and bargains for those who can withstand the pressure of the crowd flowing by.

Jump out of the main stream of traffic onto the pedestrian **Rue Caumartin** (Metro: Havre-Caumartin). There is more room to breathe on this street, bordered by smaller shops and the 18th century **St. Louis d'Antin church**. Free organ concerts are regularly scheduled on weekends; leaflets inside the main entrance give the dates. More spontaneous street music concerts are likely to be in progress at any time.

Just beyond the church, look carefully for the entrance to the **Passage du Havre**, on the left. This covered gallery is home to what may be the world's narrowest toy store, specializing in model trains. The funny, twisting passage with its glass roof looks like it leads into another century.

In fact, it leads to the Gare St. Lazare train station (Metro: St. Lazare). Turn right on Rue d'Amsterdam and walk up past Place de Budapest until you see the sign for **Androuët** on the left (N°. 41).

This small shop is known for selling the finest cheeses in Paris. There is a wonderful old-fashioned restaurant upstairs with a menu devoted to dishes with cheese in the recipe. At last count, there were about 300 varieties offered. Why not go for the

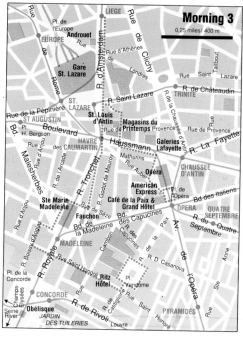

Morning 3

0.25 miles/ 400 m

Ritz Hotel, Place Vendôme

dégustation unique de tours de fromage, loosely translated as "all the cheese you can eat!" Of course, there is a good wine list to complement the savory fare.

There is a moderately-priced set menu, and luncheon *à la carte* costs between 200-300 Francs per person, depending on how many rich flavors you enjoy.

But if you're not ready to stop, or if you still haven't found what you're looking for, continue your shopping tour down Rue Tronchet and Rue Vignon, which lead from St. Lazare to the Place de la Madeleine. If there's nothing in these shops that speaks to the clothes horse in you, go back to the Salvation Army!

For unusual little gifts to bring back, we recommend **La Maison du Miel** (N°. 24 Rue Vignon), offering a variety of French honey in pretty little pots, and other products such as soaps and shampoos.

The blocky church in the center of **Place de la Madeleine** (Metro: La Madeleine) is not very welcoming. But you won't be bothered looking at it, because you'll be too busy ogling the window displays at **Fauchon**, which will leave no doubt in your mind in regard to French supremacy in the art of presenting food.

You can even have lunch *sur le pouce* (informally), a favorite of folks who work in the neighborhood: just point at what looks good to you behind the glass cases, an employee will pile it up on a plate for you and you can eat (standing up) at the counter.

Here in Paris, no one will tell on you if you eat nothing but pastry and chocolates!

Or, if you're in a picnic mood, why not head for the nearby Tuileries gardens after a stop at one of the other exotic food shops on the Place, (try **Hediard**, where they wrap your purchases in chic black and red paper and ribbon) to fill your basket with caviar, tropical fruits, and a vintage wine.

The Place is the focal point of the chic shopping district that spread across either way on **Rue Faubourg Saint Honoré** and **Rue Saint Honoré**. These streets are the traditional (if somewhat out-moded) address for major designers like **Hermès** and **Gucci**. Just around the corner is the **Place Vendôme**, elegantly symmetrical and home to the **Ritz Hotel** and **Cartier** jewelers.

If you've been an enthusiastic shopper and spent your whole day in the temples of commerce, the only fitting end is tea at the **Ritz** (proper attire required) or something stronger in the hotel's **Hemingway Bar**, named for the writer who made it his hangout.

P.M. Itineraries

1. On Top of the Town

Montmartre, perched on a steep hill on the northern rim of Paris, is a legend in itself. It seems to have its own history apart from the city below, its own famous citizens, particular traditions in entertainment and art. The Sacré-Coeur Basilica, a landmark which can be observed from all over the city, is the central tourist site, but not really the heart of its neighborhood. The spirit of Montmartre is neither religious nor monumental, but acerbic and quick-witted, rebellious and fun-loving – like many of the artists who have lived there.

Montmartre is almost always very crowded with French and foreign tourists. But, surprisingly, a walk of a few blocks away from the central **Place du Tertre** brings you to quiet streets where stairs tumble down to the city below, quiet as the cats prowling about. If stairs and steep hills are too much for you, we recommend the **Montmartroubus**, a special bus line that runs between Pigalle and the hilltop. At the cost of one Metro ticket for a one-way trip, it is the best tour deal in town. Much the same route is also covered by a miniature train (**Le Petit Train de Montmartre**); very cute, but no great improvement (and more expensive).

Start off at the **Place d'Anvers** (Metro: Anvers). Follow the signs to the *Funiculaire* that lead you up the Rue Steinkerque. The street is lined with fabric and clothes shops. If you have an eye for that sort

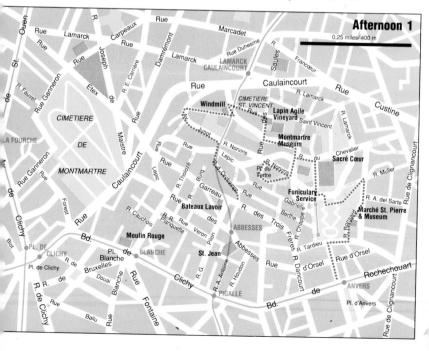

Place Suzanne - Buisson, Montmartre

of thing, there are nice bits of velvet ribbon, fancy buttons and trims, something to take home and use. You can also find lacy curtains, so typical in Paris, with unusual motifs and designs.

At the top of the street, with Montmartre's white basilica rising above you, turn right to walk down to the **Marché St. Pierre**. This 19th century covered marketplace has recently changed its vocation. It is now home to the **Primitive Art Museum** (*Musée d'Art Naïf – Max Fourny*), which presents works by artists from around the world painting in the colorful, magical style that Rousseau made famous. This small new museum also offers children's workshops, and the bookshop has an original selection of books, cards and ideas for manual activities for children. We especially like postcards which the recipient can cut out into earrings.

Above the green park bordering the Place St. Pierre looms the **Sacré-Coeur Basilica**. The 'sacred heart' church was built a mere century ago – small potatoes in this city.

Its construction came on the heels of the *Commune de Paris* a courageous uprising against Prussian domination in 1871. The uprising took its inspiration and strength from Montmartre and its anarchist population, who resisted to the last. Finally, it was French regular troops that betrayed the *Communards*, executing 25,000 of them in the final weeks of battle.

The church was built in appeasement for the bloodshed, and so has never been well-loved by local residents, known as *Montmartrois*. To this day, it is often mocked in cabaret songs on the hilltop (*La Butte*).

Climb the switchback stairway, or relax in the **Funicular railway** (use one Metro ticket) to reach the terrace in front of Sacré-Coeur. Here you have a splendid view over the city, and coin-operated telescopes to help you pick out your favorite places. Look straight out directly south into the center of

Paris, and you should easily distinguish the bright colors of Pompidou Center and the two square towers of Notre Dame. This vista is just at the opposite side of Paris from the panorama seen at the top of the Montparnasse Tower (Day 1). The Tower is off to the right, black and solitary on the skyline.

Walk around behind the church. It is like going behind a curtain and discovering a magical theater set. The **Place du Tertre** is a delightful small square filled with noise, colour, artists, easels and café tables.

Place du Tertre, Montmartre

Battling through the crowds towards the point de vue on the corner of Rue Poulbot you will find the new **Espace Montmartre** home of over 300 works of **Salvador Dali**. The museum is open every day between 10 a.m. and 7 p.m.

Stroll down Rue du Mont Cenis; leaving the crowd behind, and take a left on Rue Cortot. N° 6 was the house Eric Satie lived in while

Sacré-Coeur Basilica

Montmartre Vineyards

composing his delightful piano pieces. The painter Utrillo, who captured so many of the *Butte's* houses and cafés in his work also lived on this street, with his mother, the artist Suzanne Valdon.

At N° 12 is the **Musée de Montmartre**, settled in an 18th century manor house along with the **Montmartre Cultural Center**.

The windows look over the **Montmartre Vineyards** and Rue St. Vincent. Every October, there is a big harvest celebration in honor of this lingering reminder of more bucolic days – when windmills dotted the hillside.

Obviously, given the size of the vineyard, there is not a lot of wine bottled, and its value is more sentimental than gustatory. But it is a great source of pride to the *Montmartrois*, proving that the folks who live up here still have a strong community spirit, perhaps more than in any other part of town. On the lower floors of the museum, you can see re-creations of the study of composer and violinist Gustave Charpentier, and a typical cabaret. The graceful garden setting, the care with which original objects have been preserved and

presented, makes this the best museum to visit in Montmartre. It sums up the long history and special character of the 'village' well.

Diagonally across from the manor house and vineyards is the Montmartre Cemetery, on Rue St. Vincent. At the end of the street, turn left on Rue Girardon. The restaurant **La Maison Rose** on the corner was the subject of the painting that brought fame to Utrillo. Look out for the entrance to a small walkway on the right called the **Allée des Brouillards**. Ivy-covered gates stand before snug houses and their neat gardens. The **Château des Brouillards** (Castle of the Mists) stands opposite, in a small park. The house was built in 1772 by an actor from the Comédie Française, and several artists lived in it during the years that followed. Now boarded up and abandoned, it is a spooky place, haunted by the souls of poets, according to local legend. Continue down to Avenue Junot. Stop in the **aa galerie**, a friendly shop that has taken as its mission a revival of the artistic tradition of Montmartre. Besides showing art, they also run a music and poetry night, and dabble in theater and debate.

Take the curving avenue back up to Girardon and Rue Lepic; at the crossroads stands the **Moulin de la Galette**. The windmill was made into a dance hall

Moulin de la Galette

in the 19th century, celebrated in a painting by Renoir (and scores of others since!). Vincent van Gogh lived with his brother in a pretty little house at N° 54 Rue Lepic.

Take Avenue Junot to Rue d'Orchampt. At the end of the street there is a row of artists' studios that look much like the old **Bateau Lavoir** did when Picasso and Braque painted there. The site of their Montmartre studios is around the corner on **Place Emile Goudeau** (Metro: Abbesses).

Of course, many of the famous artists who lived and loved in Montmartre – Picasso, Apollinaire, Matisse, Toulouse-Lautrec, Maire Laurencin, to name only a few – were also great *bons vivants*. A good time is still on the agenda, and to make the most of your night out, we have three suggestions to suit your style.

Family style: Have your evening meal at **A La Mère Catherine** (on the square). This is the classic French restaurant you wish you could take home with you. The decor is dignified and warm, the menu is simple and inviting. The years haven't changed much about this place at all; it's not unusual to see three generations sitting at the same table, and no one looks out of place. (About 250 Francs per person).

Another more informal option is **Tartempion**, on Rue du Mont Cenis, serving plain fare and tasty desserts at moderate prices (100

- 150 Francs). On a warm night you can sit outdoors on the terrace with a view of the street as it abruptly ends in a stairway, and the city lights floating in space beyond.

After dinner, we suggest you stay on the *Butte* and head for **La Bohème du Tertre**. You can't miss this brightly lit cabaret on a corner of Place du Tertre. Head for the back room where musicians play perky traditional dance music (polka, waltz, and a Charleston or two). The crowd really gets going with French drinking songs and old songs about Montmartre, some of them

Transport to La Bohème du Tertre

real tear-jerkers. Order a bottle of wine and dance and sing until 2 a.m. if you choose.

Walk on the wild side: Come down off the hilltop and out of the shadow of the church to head for the naughtier regions of lower Montmartre and Pigalle. Take the twisty Rue Lepic all the way to Place Blanche (Metro: Blanche), where you find the unmistakable **Moulin Rouge**. Skip the dinner show here, the food is dull and the prices high, but take a look at the photos for fun, and buy a ticket for later if you're interested. The Moulin has been showing feathers and skin for 100 years, so they must be doing something right. Continue on down the sexy Boulevard de Clichy to the **Place de Clichy** (Metro: Place de Clichy) and the restaurant **Charlot Roi des Coquillages**. The specialty is seafood, enticingly displayed on ice out front. Of course, the French love their raw oysters, and they are

100 years of feathers, skin and sin

rumored to get the libido up, just what you need for a night in this neighborhood! The *bouillabaisse* (an intricate and hearty fish soup) has a good reputation. Count on 140-240 Francs for a full meal with wine; you have until 2 a.m. to finish it.

Also on the Place de Clichy is **Wepler**, the oyster bar and restaurant favored by author Henry Miller when he sowed his wild oats in this area. Open until 1.30 a.m., Wepler's has set menus at 135 and 230 Francs (wine not included).

After dinner, you can backtrack to Blanche and continue all the way to **Pigalle** (Metro: Pigalle), known to WWII soldiers as "Pig Alley". Along the way, there are plenty of strip shows and hawkers to lure you inside. The entrance fee to these

places is next to nothing, but the drinks served inside are obligatory and expensive.

A bit more respectable, and more of a club, is the **Folies Pigalle**, which is no longer a strip show, but a cozy music hall with very 1950s decor. A number of old strip shows have been converted this way, and Pigalle is changing its reputation. Rock clubs offer a different brand of entertainment and attract a new crowd. **La Locomotive** (90 Blvd. de Clichy) goes full steam ahead until 5.30 a.m. It is a lot bigger than the Folies, for a rowdy time in two separate discos, two bars, a video room and live music. When the club closes, you can go back up the hill for sunrise!

For Francophones only: The best way to really plunge into the spirit of Montmartre is to spend an evening at **Le Lapin Agile** (22 Rue des Saules, Metro: Lamarck-Caulaincourt). This old-fashioned cabaret just across from the Montmartre vineyards opens at 9 p.m., and the last show ends at 2 a.m. An entrance price of 110 Francs gets you a spot on a long wooden bench by a scarred table, and a little glass of cherries in *eau-de-vie*.

All night long, guests are treated to "songs, humor and poetry", in the tradition established here by Aristide Bruant. Immortalized by the Toulouse-Lautrec portrait showing him in his perpetual black hat and cape, Bruant is still present. Many of the roving performers sing songs he composed as they make the rounds of cabarets on the *Butte*. It sounds quaint, but it is also fast-paced, and a certain knowledge of French is necessary to really appreciate the "Frisky Rabbit".

So there are plenty of ways to enjoy Montmartre as Parisians do. The neighborhood goes far beyond its reputation as a touristy 'must', although there is always a fleet of

Le Lapin Agile, old-fashioned cabaret

Raw oysters at Place de Clichy

buses parked by the church, and the sound of clicking camera shutters fills the air. Yet something authentic remains, true to the spirit of the people who have lived here.

2. Sail me to the Moon

The canals of Paris? Yes indeed, and although there are no singing gondoliers, there are locks and barges, and a very particular urban landscape. What used to be a trade lifeline has now, after some years of neglect, been rejuvenated for the sake of beauty and leisure. Discover this surprising waterway, and the modern new museum complex that has been built along its banks, **Le Parc de la Villette**.

Redevelopment of the area around La Bastille began with the improvement of the **Arsenal Marina** (Metro: Bastille). The marina was once a very active commercial shipping port; adjacent to the Seine River, it joins the **Canal St. Martin** leading eastward out of the city. At Bastille, the canal goes underground, emerging again beyond Place de la République. Board the **Canauxrama Tour Boat** (Arsenal Marina, on the level of N° 50 Blvd. de la Bastille) for a three-hour journey eastward. Departures are at 9.45 a.m. and 2.30 p.m. daily.

As you glide under the city, the way is lit by sidewalk gratings sending eerie shafts of light down to the water. Classical music from the boat echoes through the tunnel.

At Quai Valmy and Quai de Jemmapes, you emerge in trees and gardens and yet another unique Parisian landscape. Wait patiently with barges at the locks; take the occasion to chat with local fishermen or admire the airy footbridges criss-crossing overhead.

On the left bank, your guide will point out the **Hôtel du Nord**. This was the setting for a popular French movie of the same name. When the hotel was recently slated for demolition, neighbors and cinephiles protested so strongly that it was eventually agreed to save the famous facade.

Near the **Bassin de la Villette**, warehouses and cafés cater to what shipping trade is left on the canal. Most of the construction dates from the 19th century. Recently, some of the industrial space has been reclaimed by artists' cooperatives as studio space and undoubtedly this neighborhood is in for some big changes in

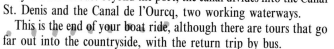

Parc de la Villette

the years ahead. Just beyond the port, the canal divides into the Canal St. Denis and the Canal de l'Ourcq, two working waterways.

This is the end of your boat ride, although there are tours that go far out into the countryside, with the return trip by bus.

What you see all around you is known as the **Parc de La Villette** (Metro: Porte de Pantin). It is a big cultural complex created in 1986 on the site of the city's former cattle market. The market building itself, a fine example of 19th century iron architecture, is now an exhibition space, **La Grande Halle**. Exhibits here range from the prestigious and often controversial Paris Biennale contemporary art show to the International Architectural Fair, and even presentations of high fashion collections. There is a small space called **La Maison de la Villette** with a permanent exhibit on the history of la Villette and the market.

Deeper in the park, the **Géode**, a polished steel sphere, looks like something from outer space that just landed in a pond. Inside, the hemispheric theater has the world's largest projection screen and dizzily slanted seating. Films made specially for these huge screens include *Man and Water, To the Limit* and *Beavers*, among others.

Reflected in the shiny steel is the **City of Science and Industry**. It takes several hours to see the whole thing, and the entrance fee (45 Francs) is relatively high, so check the scheduled closing time when you arrive. The museum is only open until 6 p.m. on Tuesday, Thursday and Friday; Wednesday un-

Arsenal Marina

til 9 p.m.; Saturday and Sunday until 8 p.m.; closed Monday. Even if you don't visit the whole thing, you can walk in the main hall for free and look at the exhibits on the ground floor. At the information windows, brochures and cassette guides in English are available.

As its official name implies, La Villette (as Parisians call it more familiarly) is devoted to science. One of the best parts is a big room for children (of all ages) where visitors have a hands-on experience with experiments using soap bubbles, mirrors, electricity, magnets and tricks of perspective. There is a jet pack simulator for armchair astronauts to fly around space with.

Other exhibits cover the universe, the origins of life; the underwater world; plant life; and there are even animal robots in a cybernetic zoo. Computer terminals at every turn inform and amuse.

Short films are shown in different areas, and the ultra-modern **Planetarium** runs several programs a day (there is an extra 15 Franc charge. Get your tickets as soon as you arrive – they go fast). In the short time it has been open, this high-tech museum has definitely become a success.

Back in the park, you see a bright red airplane aloft. This is the **Zenith Concert Hall**, which can seat up to 6,300 people. It has excellent acoustics and modern facilities, and is often booked for rock music.

The big, 137-acre (55 hectare) park is still under development. Eventually, there will be more play areas, cafés and activities. For the time being, head for the odd little building set smack in the middle of the green lawn next to the Canal de l'Ourcq. There are tables outdoors in nice weather to guide you there. Indoors, the modern decor in black and grey fits in well with the futuristic museum across the water.

City of Science and Industry

Waiters and waitresses wear floppy Bermuda shorts and bright striped socks. It has an informal atmosphere that has already made it popular for weekend brunch. On the menu: a variety of salads and grilled meats, plates of cold cuts, a hot dish of the day. Count on about 150 Francs for a meal, but there is also bar service if you just want a drink.

To get back into town from here, we suggest you board bus N° 75. Tuesday through Saturday, it stops right in front of the museum

The Géode - the world's largest projection screen

(Blvd. Macdonald, or pick it up at the Place de la Porte de Pantin, closer to the Metro and the Grande Halle).

It carries you all the way back to the center of town at the Louvre. Please remember that like most of the Parisian buses, it runs until about 8.30 p.m.; after that, you'll have to look for a taxi or use the Metro.

The route takes you past the hilly park of the **Buttes Chaumont**, built in an old quarry and planted in the English romantic style with trees, islands, and a little Greek temple just peeping through the trees atop its knoll.

Next you pass by **Place du Colonel Fabian**, and the headquarters of the French Communist Party, designed by Brazilian architect Oscar Niemeyer. You travel back down to **Place de la République** and from there turn into the Marais district and the Hôtel de Ville (Day 3). A short trip down busy **Rue de Rivoli** and the bus driver takes a break at the **Pont Neuf Bridge**.

Its name means 'New Bridge', but it is the oldest in town, and one of the most remarkable. From the riverside, note the hundreds of faces carved along the side, each one unique.

Above the bridge, the faces are unique, too, hundreds of people headed for the Latin Quarter or Les Halles. Just like you, they are off for further adventures in the Paris night.

Canal de l'Ourcq

3. The New Louvre

You may be startled to see references to the "New Louvre" or Le Grand Louvre. What happened to the old Louvre, or the Petit Louvre? The answer is: a lot! Astonishing changes have been wrought in this castle once again, not without controversy but certainly with great success. The world's largest museum is still labyrinthine, but a joy to discover for old hands as well as first-time visitors.

Le Grand Louvre is the name President François Mitterrand chose to designate his vast project of restructuring the huge palace and the museum inside. The first, much delayed step involved prizing the Finance Ministry out of its privileged digs in one wing. Those rooms are scheduled to be open to the public in 1993, when the redistribution of the collection is expected to be completed.

The second major step called on Chinese-American architect I.M. Pei to create a new entrance and orientation center.

His design is already world-famous, and will certainly become part of the architectural legend of Paris. The large glass **Pyramid** rises in the middle of the **Cour Napoléon**. Around it, three smaller pyramids. The area between them is accented by flat, triangular basins in dark stone, raised slightly above the level of the ground. Fountains in these pools complete the composition.

The "landscape", as Pei calls it, in the tradition of landscape artist Le Nôtre, was designed to bring light into the museum entrance below, and it also succeeds in lightening the whole courtyard and the stone façades surrounding it.

The thoughtful use of materials and colors allows the sky and water to become elements in the illusionistic space. The glass was specially developed and manufactured by St. Gobain, polished twice in France and England. It is held in place by stainless steel nodes and

The Pyramid, Le Grand Louvre

cables. The result is light and sparkling, a balance of reflection and transparency weighed against the thick stone façade, heavy with centuries of history.

Go through the revolving door and turn down the spiral staircase. The central pillar there is an ingenious elevator. This is the **Hall Napoléon** reception area. The din of milling visitors manages not to be overbearing, and there is plenty of space for the crowd.

The new museum services located here are excellent. Ticket windows, the information desk, a bookshop, the rest rooms, and the cafeteria are all easy to find and reach – already a big improvement over the "old" Louvre! A sit-down restaurant and a sandwich bar provide other alternatives for hungry and thirsty visitors. A bank of computers lists the day's exhibits and activities, and rooms which may be temporarily closed. You will also find a bank, a post office, a cloak room and even an infirmary on this level.

When construction began, major archaeological research was carried out. The fruit of these efforts is now on display in a big underground exhibition area called "the Medieval Louvre". Another castle has thus been opened beneath the famed palace-museum above. Drawings and scale models show the Louvre at different stages of its career, and reveal how many transformations it had known prior to today.

Walk around the ancient walls and most of the medieval fortress, past the towers that were once the gates to the city. The well-designed rooms travel through time. Beautifully lit, quiet and pleasant to walk through, they are a fantastic discovery which allows us to grasp the span of history encompassed by the leviathan. The architectural prowess used to display the old foundations so effectively is a marvel.

There is an exhibition of some of the artifacts uncovered, including many ceramic pieces. The most splendid find was certainly the **Helmet of Charles VI**, found in barely recognizable bits and artfully reproduced here. It is on display in the **Salle Saint Louis**, perhaps the most breathtaking part of the newly opened area. Built around 1240, the vaulted ceiling was flattened by construction in the 16th century, but it still conjures up an image of the castle that was.

The Louvre, with these new openings and additions, is now bigger than ever, and it is still impossible not to get lost in the many rooms and corridors. No matter which way you turn, you always seem to end up in the Egyptian Antiquities! However, like Alice in Wonder-

land, visitors need only wander as circumstance leads to discover many marvels. The presence of the Pyramid, which you may see from different angles as you pass the tall windows, is of some help in orientation.

On the ground floor, the **Oriental, Egyptian, Greek and Roman Antiquities** were the first items to be displayed in the museum. Many were brought back from Napoléon's campaigns. One remarkable pieces is **Hammurabi's Code**, from ancient Babylon.

The Egyptian section has, of course, mummies and cult objects, busts and statues of ancient rulers. This famous collection enables scholars to trace the whole development of Egyptian civilization from prehistory to the Christian era. The new Pyramid seems even more fitting when considered in light of these rooms.

Two very famous ladies grace the Greek and Roman rooms: *Venus de Milo* and *Winged Victory*. Their celebrity has somewhat overshadowed the rest of the collection, rich and varied. Vast, sunny and quiet, the proportions of the rooms are well suited to the pieces.

Although the outstanding part of this section is made up of sculpture, there are also bronzes, decorative and useful objects, tools, jewelry and bas-reliefs. Certainly the traces of classical influence remain present in much of the architecture of Paris, and here is a chance to get an eyeful of the original product.

The second major section of the Louvre collection is **paintings**. These are from all the European schools, from the 13th to the 17th centuries, and they are displayed on the upper floors.

Two-thirds of the paintings are French, and include works by 17th-18th century great artists such as de la Tour, Poussin, Watteau

Do you smile to greet a lover ...?

and Fragonard; all to be visited in the **Grande Galerie**.

This section's most famous resident is, of course, the *Mona Lisa*, in the company of an impressive gathering of other works by Leonardo da Vinci. Masterpieces by Raphael, Titian, and Veronese compete for the visitor's eye in these rooms where the walls seem to glow and radiate energy.

Other crowd-stoppers are the large paintings in the **Pavillon Denon**, including *Napoléon Crowning Josephine* (David), *The Great Odalisque* (Ingres), *The Raft of the Medusa* (Géricault), and the famous revolutionary and inspiring painting of *Liberty Leading the People* (Delacroix).

The third section is known as **Objets d'Art**, and includes furniture, jewelry and small statuary, much of it confiscated from royalty at the time of the Revolution. **Apollo's Gallery** is a beautiful room with an intricate ceiling painted by Delacroix. Glass cases display the remaining pieces of the Crown Jewels of France. The reputed crown of St. Louis sits besides Napoléon's coronation headgear. Numerous gem-encrusted and golden objects glitter beneath the guard's watchful eye. Less overwhelming, but just as admirable, is the extensive collection of tapestries, furniture and clocks from various periods.

The great redistribution of paintings in the Louvre, now that more space is available, will take several years to complete. Eventually, paintings will be rearranged in a more chronological perspective, and according to national schools. But already, works which were previously not hung for lack of space can be discovered. In the new top-floor rooms, these include *The History of Alexander* by Le Brun, a series of huge paintings that have been rolled up for almost 30 years. Other works will be shown on a rotating basis, as the program of redistribution is carried out.

The main entrance to the museum is through the Pyramid (Metro: Palais Royal), but you may be able to dodge a line by using the Richelieu Passage, off Rue de Rivoli and the Place du Palais Royal. It is open daily, except Tuesday, from 9 a.m. to 6 p.m. and Wednesday and Monday until 10 p.m.

English cassette tours are available, and there is a six-minute film presentation of some of the major works which can be viewed in the reception area. You may also take a tour with a guide.

Restaurant, money exchange and post office facilities are handy, and the bookshop is unbelievable. Elegant and practical, it contains not only postcards and prints, but 15,000 books and periodicals in many languages. They also sell casts of art works, jewelery and other gift items.

The drafty, dim, dusty Louvre is dead! Long live the New Louvre!

Nightlife

There is plenty to do in Paris after the streetlights blink on, which is wonderfully late in the day during the early summer months. Part of the fun is discovering the many beautiful aspects of the city under dark skies, decked out in her jewels of light. The view along the riverside, or from high atop the Eiffel Tower, is enchanting.

Tours: There are three tour companies along the Seine. The **Vedettes du Pont Neuf**, entrance under the bridge near St. Michel and Notre Dame, leave every 30 minutes until 5 p.m. Monday to Thursday, and until 10 p.m. the rest of the week. The trip takes about an hour and powerful spotlights illuminate the bridges and buildings as you go. The same tours are run by **Bateaux Mouches** at Pont d'Alma, although less frequently. Across from the Eiffel Tower at the Pont d'Iéna are **Les Bateaux Parisiens**. The ride costs 35 Francs, lunch cruise about 300 Francs, and dinner around 550 Francs.

Bateaux Mouches

The famous Pigalle

Nocturnal bus tours pass spendidly illuminated monuments of the city. Some tours end at the Moulin Rouge for French can-can and champagne, or the Lido on the Champs-Elysées. Two well-known tours in town are **Paris Vision** (214 Rue de Rivoli 75001) and **Cityrama** (4 Place des Pyramides 75001); their packages are also sold in many agencies, especially around the Opéra. The basic price is between 30 and 50 Francs, and goes up depending on add-ons such as lunch, dinner or a show. The companies also organize day trips outside town to some popular sites like Versailles and Chartres.

For a really special night tour, rent a **chauffeured limousine**. You can even have a telephone in the car to call the folks back home! For bilingual chauffeurs and a 24-hour reservation service, try **Paris Major Limousine**.(Tel: 42.45.34.14), **Murdoch Associés**, (Tel: 47.20.00.21), or **MLG Maurice Letirand** (Tel: 40.53.00.21).

Stage: Tickets to the ballet, opera, concert, or a theater production can be bought at an agency or at the theater. The FNAC Stores (music and books) around town (a big store in the Forum des Halles shopping center) sell tickets to most concerts. For the theater, go to the Kiosque de la Madeleine, a big ticket booth in the middle of Place de la Madeleine. You can buy half--price tickets on the day of performance, but you had best arrive before noon to do so.

Complete weekly listings, in the *Official des Spectacles* and other magazines. Also look at the distinctive green 'Morris Columns'. The late nineteenth century design is by an English artist, and his dark green kiosks splashed with posters.

Jazz clubs: Paris loves jazz and clubs seem to have undergone a renaissance recently. Check the *Official* to see what's on in the following clubs:

New Morning
7-9 Rue des Petits Ecuries (75010)

Big, scznt decor, tucked in a back alley. Good acoustics. Some greats keep coming back, including Richie Havens, Taj Mahal, Wayne Shorter, Stan Getz and Prince. Very informal and hip, for serious music lovers.

Bar Lionel Hampton
Hotel Meridian
81 Blvd. Gouvion-St. Cyr (75017)

A favorite with performaners and fans. Seats several hundred. Run by a local jazz hero known simply as Moustache, who shows some of the finest jazz musicians, such as Harry Edison, Oscar Peterson, Memphis Slim and Benny Carter the respect they deserve. Not a night owl? Enjoy jazz here on Sunday, over brunch.

Le Petit Journal
71 Blvd. St. Michel (75005) and **Le Petit Journal Montparnasse**, 13 Rue du Commandant-Mouchotte (75014)

Same owners, different styles. The first features Dixieland and Swing, the second contemporary: Herbie Hancock, Art Blakey and Stéphane Grappelli. Both good food and good vibes.

After-Hours Clubs
Clubs in Paris tend to be very 'clubby' subjecting would-be partiers to heavy scrutiny at the door. No grubby clothes, so dress fashionably, and don't forget to bring plenty of money. For all sorts of adventures:

Les Bains Douches
7 Rue du Bourg-l'Abbé (75003)

Old public bath house, the gathering place of fashion victims and the young and hip. To be sure of getting in, make a reservation to eat at the restaurant first (Tel: 48.87.0.80).

Le Tango
13 Rue au Maire (75003)

A meeting place for African sapeurs, guys who spend fantastic sums of money on incredible-looking clothes. A wild time in store, if you're dressed right!

Le Garage
41 Rue Washington (75008)

Not far from the Champs-Elysées. A little more low-key. Current hits and retro music, a light show. A favorite of more mature customers.

Le Palace
8 Rue FBG, Montmartre (75009)

Occasional live music events, two big dance floors and bars. One of the most popular clubs in town, with a variety of "theme" nights and plenty of local stars.

Day Trips

Short Excursions

Most visitors to Paris enjoy at least one excursion out of the city, to tour a famous site or get a peek at the French countryside. The region around the city is called the *Ile de France*, rich in history and culture. Some of the most popular spots are also the most accessible. The following destinations can easily be reached and visited in a day. If you leave Paris before noon, you can be back in time for dinner.

1. Penultimate Palace

Versailles is top on the list of what tourists want to see outside of the city. Rapid transit line RER C, with stops all along the left bank of the Seine River, takes you there in a jiffy. When you exit at the Versailles station, signs clearly indicate how to walk or take a bus to the castle, a short distance away.

The inside of the palace is open daily, except Monday, from 9.30 a.m. to 5.30 p.m., and the vast gardens are open from morning to nightfall. A guided tour of the palace (unaccompanied visits are not allowed) takes about an hour, but you may have to wait in line almost that long beforehand.

Versailles

It took 50 years to complete Louis XIV's plans for the sumptuous palace that gives meaning to the word *grandeur*. This insensate display of wealth foreshadowed the French Revolution. Because he hated Paris and the unpredictable Parisians, and was jealous of the luxury castle at Vaux-le-Vicomte built by his finance minister, the young monarch planned his opulent château well west of the city. He changed the very landscape to create his gardens, and installed an elaborate system of pumps to bring water from the Seine to his fountains.

More than 1,000 members of court lived in the attic rooms, and life in the microcosm was as far removed from the life outside the palace walls as they could make it. Such daily events as 'the King's Rise' (remember he was known as the 'Sun King') took on momentous importance for the coterie.

Although revolutionary outrage emptied the castle of most of the furnishings, it has slowly been restored and pieces donated by foreign countries or collected and purchased in France have helped to fill out the many rooms in a style approaching the original splendor.

In the precise center of the palace lie the **Royal Apartments**. The small staircase linking the King's sitting room to the Queen's was added by Louis XV and his mistress, Madame de Pompadour. Look for the secret passage later used by Louis XVI's wife, Marie Antoinette, to escape the rabble barging through the gates. That escape is the supposed occasion of her infamous reply to the people's cry for bread: "Let them eat cake" (*Qu'ils mangent de la brioche*). Historians cast doubt on her actual words, but certainly the sentiment is clear. Poverty and suffering were, perhaps, beyond her imagination, just as the opulence she took for granted is beyond our own.

The great **Hall of Mirrors** was used as a royal reception and ball room. More recently, the Treaty of Versailles ending WWI was signed there. Another historical event, which the French are less

wont to recall, took place in 1871: the proclamation of the German Empire.

The pint-size **Opera House**, built for Louis XV, is a sumptuous hall which once again welcomes special performances, thanks to recent restoration.

Outdoors, the park was designed by André le Nôtre, who created the image of the royal garden *à la française*. Three more residences dot the landscape. The **Grand Trianon**, on the bank of the Grand Canal, was built by Louis XIV. He sought peace within its pink marble walls, away from the crowd at court. The **Petit Trianon** was built by his successor, but mainly enjoyed by the last of the Louis, the ill-fated number XVI. Queen Marie Antoinette preferred the **Hameau**, a make-believe hamlet, where she played milkmaid with fine porcelain milk pails.

In the form of a *fleur-de-lys* (symbol of royalty), the **Grand Canal**

Le Hameau

Chartres

stretches out from the foot of the terrace, dividing the wooded park in two. The two large fountains in the central alley are the **Latona** and **Apollo** fountains. The first is a weird amphibian allegory dominating the *Tapis Vert*, the central lawn. The second represents the god driving a chariot led by powerful horses.

Both sides of the park are studded with delightful groves, ponds, exotic bushes, ancient trees and velvety grass. The fountains are so numerous that even a king's coffers couldn't keep them going nowadays, but on the first and third Sundays of June through September, all gush again, their musical splashing joining birdsong in the air. Occasional evening festivities come complete with fireworks and multi-colored lights. All in all, the fame of this majestic site is well-deserved. As the French saying has it, it is worth the detour.

2. Country Cathedral: Chartres

Mostly visited for its **Gothic Cathedral**, the old town is a pleasant and relaxing place to explore. A world away from the big-city mentality of Paris, Chartres is just 60 miles (97 km) southwest, an

Rose Window, Cathedral of Chartres

hour's train ride from Montparnasse station.

The medieval town sits upon a plateau hemmed in by wheatfields on the banks of the Eure River. The cathedral's spires rise high above the rich plain to welcome you, as they have welcomed pilgrims since the 13th century. It is a short walk uphill from the SNCF train station to the site.

Extensive restoration work has long kept the Cathedral of Chartres sheathed in scaffolding, but it does not deter from the beauty of the **Rose Windows** viewed from the inside. Their fame is due to both beauty and age, for they date from the 12th and 13th centuries, among the oldest examples of this type of religious art to be found in the world. These unique stained-glass masterpieces survived a disastrous fire in 1149 (most of the previous Romanesque cathedral was destroyed), the French Revolution, and two world wars (the windows were removed and stored away during WWII).

The 'Chartres blue' color, a rich, deep tone, is not found elsewhere and apparently cannot be duplicated. Some of the panes seem lighter in color than others, the result of an experimental restoration. Light passing through these windows colors the floor, joining the traces of the ancient marble **Labyrinth** set in the nave. The labyrinth is symbolic of Christian pilgrimages of the early Middle Ages.

Visit the **Crypt** to see the site of an even more ancient ritual. The cathedral was built on the grounds of a Druid worship place. You can see a wall of ancient paintings dating from Gallo-Roman times (4th century and 12th century). Guided tours of the largest and one of the most beautiful crypts in France start from the Maison des Clercs, opposite the south side of the cathedral.

As you leave the cathedral, look up at the two Romanesque towers. The left tower, though known as the 'New Tower', is actually the older, but the delicate Gothic spire atop was added on later, in the 16th century. The thicker spire on the right tower is from the earlier Romanesque period. Here is a good opportunity to observe the difference between these two styles of architecture, so widely present in France.

Behind the cathedral is the **Musée des Beaux Arts**, housing a collection of tapestries, enamels and paintings from the Renaissance through the 18th century. There is also a room devoted to the history of the town.

Below the terraced garden behind the museum runs the Eure River. It travels past the **Eglise Saint André**, a Romanesque church in poor

repair. Follow the pathway along the river, past the traditional wash houses and the remains of the old city wall, all the way to the **Place Saint Pierre**. There another set of magnificent stained-glass windows awaits you in the church.

Most of the old town is a protected site, and has been well-restored and improved with pedestrian areas. It is also a lively agricultural center and capital of the Beauce region. You can tour the city with an experienced guide. For information on this and other possibilities, and for maps, books and brochures, stop in at the tourist office on Rue du Cloître Notre-Dame, right alongside the cathedral.

3. Garden of Delights

The final suggestion for a short day trip takes you into the region of Normandy. Peaceful fields and forests lie waiting for you just a short distance northwest of Paris. Add a note of adventure to your trip by setting out on a bike; the SNCF train company offers a good deal on rental right at the station. But however you go, take a deep breath of the fragrant countryside and let yourself be transported.

It's a little more difficult to reach **Giverny** than the previous

Monet's house

destinations, but well worth the effort. Take a train from the Gare St. Lazare to Vernon. It is about a one hour trip. At the station, you can take a taxi or hop on a bike for the trip to **Claude Monet's House and Garden**.

The pink and green house itself is an explosion of color, more daring than most decorators would attempt. The dining room, for example, is bright yellow, lined with priceless chinaware plates. The kitchen is a soaring sky blue. The walls of the artist's rooms are generously hung with Japanese prints from his extensive and beautiful collection.

The gardens are Monet's paintings come to life, or his paintings are his gardens come to art. The green foliage contrasts with luminous flowers representing hundreds of varieties. Here are the water-lilies, the Japanese bridge, the willow and the pond – so many of the subjects of his impressionist works.

Giverny is very popular on summer afternoons, so start out early on a weekday (not Monday) to get the most pleasure from your visit.

The Seine River meets the Epte here, and there are pretty spots for picnics. If you have a car, continue northwest to **Lyons la Forêt**, a village set in a beech tree forest. Potted geraniums decorate the windows of typical Normandy half-timber facades. Otherwise, right in Vernon, try the Restaurant de la Poste. The fare is simple and inexpensive, and the portions are sized for hearty country appetites.

Long Excursions

Here are two destinations to take you out of the traffic and pulse of present-day life. Get out of your Paris hotel early in the morning and wake up slowly on the train carrying you out of the urban sprawl and into the fresh air and green fields. In the mighty forest of Compiègne, Napoléon and his Empress Eugénie retired to hunt and fish. On the fortified hilltop at Provins, gaze out of the medieval watchtower as guards did centuries ago, at the plain rolling away on all sides.

4. Majestic Woodlands

Compiègne is located north of Paris in a region which takes its name from the principal river, the Oise. You can reach it by train from the Gare du Nord station in about one hour. Visit the historic city and the majestic forest, where several attractions await you. A very enjoyable tour can be made either by SNCF bus, or on a bike (rentals at the station). The bike trails are excellent; the farthest site, Pierrefonds, is at a distance of about 10 miles (16 km).

The **Town of Compiègne** began as a Roman outpost. A long series of royal residents was to follow. It was here, in 1430, that Joan of

Arc, on a campaign to free the city under siege, was captured by her enemies.

The town center is across the Oise River from the train station. Walk straight down the main street leading off the bridge (Rue Solférino) to the **Place St. Jacques**. This brings you directly in front of the town's most remarkable monument, the **Hôtel de Ville**. The building is in the late Gothic style, elaborately decorated with figures and cornices. Just above the main door, Louis XII parades on a horse. High atop the central tower, three jolly fellows in bright pantaloons strike the hour. The bell they strike dates from 1303, making it the oldest one in France.

The town hall, also the main tourist office for Compiègne, offers excellent information about the town and forest, provides maps, and can arrange for tours and guides.

Take the street across the square, Rue St. Corneille, to discover the ruins of a beautiful old abbey. The cloisters are still standing, with a lovely promenade under vaulted ceilings.

Behind the cloisters, there is a pedestrian area lined with shops and restaurants. Continue up Rue de Lombards. Pass the old salt house (*Grenier à Sel*) on your right and a little further on, notice the house inscribed **La Vieille Cassine**. This is the only house of the 15th century half-timber style remaining in town.

Now walk past **St. Jacques Church** on your right (or stop in at the sculpted wood inside), up Rue du Dahomey and into the **Parc du Palais**.

Here is a sweeping view up a long slow rise leading into the forest. The central alley stretches 3 miles (5 km) to the crown of the hill, **Les Beaux Konts**. Napoléon Bonaparte designed this clearing in 1910 to remind his second wife, Marie-Louise, of her Austrian homeland.

You can visit the **Palais** (closed Tuesday), built in the 18th century, and restored by Napoléon. In addition to furnishings and souvenirs from the First and Second Empire, the

Palais houses a **Car Museum**, with more than 150 models.

The **Forest of Compiègne** opens up another realm. Typically, a tour takes you through tall, straight trees to several different destinations. The closest is the **Armistice Clearing**. On this spot the 1918 Armistice between France and Germany was signed. A railroad car has been placed on the site, complete with wax figures re-enacting the scene. Attached to the car is a photo museum devoted to WWI. Viewing through stereoscopes, visitors flip through the impressive collection of life in the trenches, parade uniforms, the different fronts. If you are interested in that historical period, or in the history of photography, don't miss this little gem of an exhibit, tucked away in the woods.

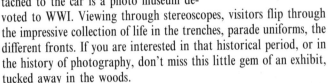

The Forest of Compiègne

The next stop is the village of **Vieux Moulins** and the fishing ponds called the **Etangs de Saint Pierre**. A favorite spot for afternoon strolls, the village also boasts a fine inn and restaurant, the **Auberge de la Bonne Idée**.

Your final destination in the forest is the village and castle of **Pierrefonds**. The pretty little town sits on the banks of a lake formed by the waters of the Berne River. Above it towers the **Château**, an enormous fortress built in 1400, almost completely dismantled in later centuries, and finally reconstructed by Violet-le-Duc for Napoléon III (closed Tuesday). The defences of the castle are interesting and the stylized decoration evokes a cloak-and-dagger Middle Ages. In fact, the architect imposed his own extremely personal ideas of medieval design on the restoration, and the result, as you will see, is rather surprising.

The gilded bees and hunting frescos recall Napoléon III and the Second Empire. The castle became government property when Napoléon fell from power. It is said that the former Empress Eugénie visited the castle with a group of tourists in 1912.

Town Hall, Compiègne

When she reached the Emperor's bedroom, she wept.

Return to Compiègne under the leafy canopy. For centuries, French royalty has taken this path and, leaving behind the rich hunting grounds and peaceful forest, headed back to the fractious city of Paris with a small sigh of regret.

5. Euro Disney Resort

Finally, after several years of publicity, the much talked about Euro Disney Resort opens its doors to the general public on 12 April 1992. This is only the first stage in a development which is scheduled to continue until 2017, when it is estimated that this children's dream-world will cover an area one fifth the size of Paris.

The complex is situated 20 miles (32km) east of Paris and can be reached by either car or RER train (Line A) from central Paris at

Auber, Châtelet or Étoile. Marne-la-Vallée is the name of the railway station at Euro Disney and it will be linked up to the high-speed TGV rail network in 1994.

Entrance to the Park costs 225 francs for adults, 150 francs for children under 12 years of age. A day trip will cost a family of four (two adults and two children) 750 francs excluding meals and, if you travel by car, parking fees. For information and to make reservations in one of the six hotels phone (1) 49.41. 49.10 in Paris, or (71) 753 2900 in London.

Sleeping Beauty's Castle

Euro Disneyland will be similar in structure to its sister parks in Florida and California. The Resort initially will comprise one theme park, six hotels, an entertainment centre, a convention centre and a golf course. A second park and film studios will open in the mid-1990s. The five imaginary worlds which make up Euro Disneyland today include Fantasyland, Discoveryland, Main Street USA representing the early 1900s with ragtime and Dixieland bands, Frontierland (which needs little expla-

Disneyland Hotel

nation but surely will be essential for most jaded commuters and their sons), and finally Adventureland representing the mysteries of an African-like continent. There is no doubt that this immense resort, just under an hour from the centre of Paris, will become a major tourist attrraction just as its parent has done in Florida.

The gang's all here

Dining

It would take years to sample all the restaurants in Paris, and a staff to keep up with changes and openings. Parisians enjoy eating out of their favorite *bistro* as much as discovering a new restaurant or having a night out in a really fine establishment. Take the suggestions given in each itinerary in this book, or walk into a place that looks (and smells) great, or just try the restaurants listed below. Addresses include the *code postal*, or zip code; the last two numbers indicate the district (*arrondissement*). Prices are based on the set price menu, if there is one, or a three-course *à la carte* meal for one person, with a moderately-priced wine.

Many restaurants close on Sunday. Reservations are required in expensive restaurants, and highly recommended on Friday and Saturday nights for moderate restaurants.

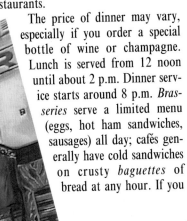

The price of dinner may vary, especially if you order a special bottle of wine or champagne. Lunch is served from 12 noon until about 2 p.m. Dinner service starts around 8 p.m. *Brasseries* serve a limited menu (eggs, hot ham sandwiches, sausages) all day; cafés generally have cold sandwiches on crusty *baguettes* of bread at any hour. If you

Experiences

want a superb gourmet experience, try lunchtime, rather than dinner, when many expensive places offer set menus that can be real savings over *à la carte*.

Expensive restaurants

Dinner with a moderately-priced wine costs at least 500 Francs per person, probably more. Lunch is much cheaper, especially for set menus; a good way to savor delectable dishes at affordable prices.

La Tour d'Argent. 15 Quai de la Tournelle (75005).
Tel: 43.54.23.31. *Closed on Monday.* Credit cards: VISA, AE, DC.
Famous for the view of Notre Dame as well as recipes based on duck. The service is impeccable, the decor divine. Dinner, expect minimum 900 Francs.

Lasserre. Ave. Franklin Roosevelt (75008). Tel: 43.59.53.43.
Closed on Sunday, Monday lunch, August. No credit cards accepted.
In the summer, you dine under the stars when they roll back the ceiling upstairs. Incredible wine list, dishes rather delicate. Just using the extravagant cutlery is half the pleasure. Around 700 Francs.

Chez Jamin. 32 Rue de Longchamp (75016). Tel: 47.27.12.27.
Closed on weekends, and in July. Credit cards: VISA, AE, DC.
A gastronomic *ne plus ultra*, specializing in *nouvelle cuisine*. Reservations are accepted eight weeks in advance! The menu is about 980 Francs, excluding wine, per person.

Arpège. 84 Rue de Varenne (75007).
Tel: 45.51.47.33. and **45.51.20.02.** *Closed Sunday lunch, Saturdays and end of July until 21st August.* Credit cards: VISA, AE, DC.

This superb restaurant is among the top 12 in Paris and can be recommended. The cellar is as one would expect – good but not expensive. Between 500 and 900 Francs, excluding wine.

Moderate restaurants

There is an abundance of restaurants in this category, where a meal for one with wine costs between 150 and 300 Francs. Here are a few favorites that are not included in the itineraries:

Le Bar des Théâtres. 6 Ave. Montaigne (75008).
Tel: 47.23.34.63. *Open daily.* Credit card: VISA.

This busy, noisy place has been around for 40 years, serving tasty and traditional French food in a friendly atmosphere. Don't mind the napkins, and keep away if you hate cigarette smoke – but this place typifies the kind of restaurant that used to make people say it was just about impossible to get a bad meal in France.

Chez Ma Cousine. 12 Rue Norvins (75018).
Tel: 46.06.49.35. *Open daily.* Credit cards: VISA, AE, DC, MC.

In Montmartre, right on the Place du Tertre, this small and friendly place also offers a cabaret in the evening, and a *crêpe* stand on the street.

Terminus Nord. 23 Rue de Dunkerque (75010).
Tel: 42.85.05.15. *Open daily.* Credit cards: VISA, AE, DC.
Just across from the Gare du Nord train station, this big, busy brasserie has a 1925 decor and a staff of very professional waiters. Hearty portions for healthy appetites, traditional French food including seafood specials, excellent beef and lamb dishes.

Auberge de Jarente. 7 Rue de Jarente (75004).
Tel: 43.54.78.06. *Closed Sunday, Monday and in August.* Credit cards: VISA, AE, DC.
Small welcoming restaurant specialising in Basque dishes. The uncomplicated cuisine makes a welcome change. Try the *piperade de St. Jean* and *gâteau Basque*.

La Citrouille. 10 Rue Grégoire de Tours (75006).
Tel: 43.29.90.41. *Open daily.*
In the heart of the Latin Quarter near Odéon, the restaurant serves fresh salads and simple well-prepared dishes at low prices – a nice escape from steak and French fries!

Le Poète Ivre. 8 Rue Leopold (75002).
Tel: 40.26.26.46. *Closed Sundays.* Credit cards: VISA.
One of the best Thai restaurants in town. It is quite small but well known so it would be wise to book if you plan to visit on Friday or Saturday. Situated in an old and quiet part of Paris.

Nos Ancêtres les Gaulois. 39 Rue Saint Louis en l'Ile (75004).
Tel: 46.33.66.07. *Open nightly.* Credit cards: CB, DC, AE, VISA.
On the chic island of St. Louis right in the center of town, Nos Ancêtres has a reputation for being unique, based more on the ambience than the food. The menu mainly offers grilled meats and the hearty portions are served with strong wine by Gaulish characters in winged helmets. Good value and good fun.

Inexpensive restaurants

For around 150 Francs per person, you can have the pleasure of a good French meal and wine at the following addresses:

Chartier. 7 Rue du Faubourg Montmartre (75009).
Tel: 47.70.86.29. *Closed on Sunday.*
Near the Opéra, the best-known low-price eatery in town. The ambience is an experience in itself: turn-of-the-century decor, snappy waiters, shared tables and plenty of *bonhommie*. Arrive before 2 p.m. in the afternoon or 9.30 at night, or you probably won't get a seat.

Polidor. 41 Rue Monsieur-le-Prince (75006). *Closed on Sunday, Monday and in August.*

Long favored by students and professors, this Latin Quarter hangout offers home-style cooking and art-deco design. Everything is very relaxed, including the service, and no gastronomic miracles are in order, but Hemingway ate here, and so can you.

Le Lazare. 68 Rue Quincampoix 75003. *Open evenings from 7 p.m. to 12.30 a.m. Closed on Sunday and Monday.*

Mr. Toyre, the current owner of this mellow restaurant, was born in the same year that his parents opened their establishment. His wife now works at the stove, cooking up hearty French dishes (the four-course menu with wine is just 105 Francs) and a *bouillabaisse* special (175 Francs including wine). Very quiet and friendly, this lovely place has weathered the neighborhood's many changes with dignity and charm.

Pastavino. 6 Rue Pierre Lescot (75001), 59 Rue Dauphine (75006) and 30 Rue Passy (75016)

One inside the Forum des Halles shopping center; one on the street leading off the Pont Neuf at the tip of the Ile de la Cité; and one in the 16th, make three branches of this Italian restaurant and take-away which serves salads, pasta dishes and tasty desserts at unbeatable prices.

A few bars and wine bars

L'Ecluse. 15 Quai des Grands-Augustins (75006), Rue Mondétour (75001), Rue de la Roquette (75011), Place de la Madeleine (75008), Rue François 1er (75008).
All branches are closed on Sunday.
The grand-daddy of Parisian wine bars. Rather expensive, but an outstanding selection of Bordeaux wines by the glass or bottle, and an appetizing choice of simple foods to accompany them.

Le Rubis. 10 Rue du Marché St. Honoré (75001).
Closed on weekends and in August.
This is the place to be when the *Beaujolais Nouveau* comes out in October, and the party fills up the whole street. In other seasons, it is a nice place for lunch and to have a glass of something divine.

Villi's. Rue des Petits Champs (75001). *Closed on Sunday.*
Near the chic shopping on Place des Victoires, Villi's specializes in
Côte du Rhône wines, served with light meals.

Rosebud. 11 bis Rue Delambre (75014). *Open till 2 a.m. or later.*
This Montparnasse bar is a well-known nocturnal watering-hole.

La Rhumerie. 166 Blvd. St. Germain (75006)
A popular bar that specializes in punches of every flavor.

Harry's Bar. 5 Rue Daunou (75002)
We couldn't leave this one out – famous around the world, Harry's
opened in 1911, was second home to Hemingway, and the Bloody
Mary was created there. Still popular and plenty of characters to
check out until the wee early hours.

Regulations – Duty Free

U.S. residents may bring back $400 worth of merchandise per traveler for personal use or as gifts, before paying a flat 10% tax on additional value up to $1,000. Included in this allowance is 1 liter (1 quart) of alcohol per traveler over age 21 and one bottle of U.S.-trademarked perfume. There is no tax on art or antiques more than 100 years old. Families may pool their declarations, provided that no similar ones have been made in the preceding 30-day period.

Canadian residents have a $300 yearly limit, in addition to the 50 cigars, 200 cigarettes, 2 pounds of tobacco and 40 ounces of alcohol they may bring in tax free.

EEC countries are on the verge of declaring an open border policy, accompanied by the standardization of VAT taxes. Until then, goods must be declared as: (a) goods from a shop in an EEC country or (b) goods from outside the EEC or from a duty-free shop in an EEC country. In category (a) you may import duty free: 300 cigarettes or 150 cigarillos or 50 cigars or 400 grams of tobacco; 1 ½ liters of alcoholic beverages over 22% vol. (38.8 proof) or 3 liters of under 22% vol. (including sparkling, fortified or still table wine); 4 liters of still wine; 75 grams of perfume; 13 ounces of toilet water, additional goods up to a value of 25%.

In category (b) you may import duty free: 200 cigarettes or 100 cigarillos or 50 cigars or 400 grams of tobacco; 1 liter of alcoholic beverages over 22% vol. (38.8 proof) or 2 liters of under 22% vol. (including sparkling, fortified or still table wine); 2 liters of still wine; 50 grams of perfume; 9 ounces of toilet water; additional goods up to a value of £32.

Of course, *no animals or pets may be brought into the U.K.* – and this rule is strictly enforced.

Duty-free Shops, found in the airports and on the planes themselves, are not always the cheapest places to shop. The mark-up (as

much as 100 to 200 percent) overwhelms the tax savings, and you are better off getting your duty-free goods directly from a shop in town, if you can.

The other alternative is to get the VAT tax refunded at the airport. First of all, your purchases in a single store must amount to 1,200 Francs for non-EEC residents; for EEC residents, tax can be refunded only on single items with a value of at least 2,000 Francs. The store must fill out a special form (make sure it corresponds to your place of residence inside or outside the EEC). You must include banking information on the form, because refunds are only paid directly into accounts. As you leave France, customs officials will ask for the forms, and look at the goods, so arrive with plenty of time to go through this process.

In general, it is not worth the hassle to seek a refund this way, unless you've got a big item to declare. But beware of customs officials on the arrival end, who may decide to slap a tax on you there, especially if you are returning to an EEC country!

Alcohol and perfumes

If you want to purchase **Alcoholic Beverages**, we suggest you stick with liqueurs, aperitifs or champagnes. A good wine may suffer from transportation and end up disappointing you. Major supermarkets have the best prices and a satisfactory selection; luxury shops on the Place de la Madeleine offer high-quality items in gift packages.

Perfumes are another favorite, but the prices are only interesting if you are able to purchase them tax-free. This means you should have your plane ticket and passport with you when you go to the shop. Only certain shops offer an instant refund on tax. In addition to Galeries Lafayette and Printemps department stores, two other boutiques in the Opéra district offer this service: **Michel Swiss** and

Raoul & Curly; the first is right on the Place de l'Opéra (16 Rue de la Paix) and the other is just down the street at 47 Ave. de l'Opéra.

Beauty and fashion

Fashion is synonymous with Paris, and just looking at Parisians makes you want to dress up yourself. The venerable *couture* houses are on **Avenue Montaigne** (Morning #1) and **Faubourg St. Honoré** (Morning #3). For less classic and more affordable attire, try around Saint Germain (Day #1), or head for the shops of up-and-coming designers **Sonia Rykiel** or **Claude Montana**, both on Rue de Grenelle, numbers 6 and 31, respectively (Metro: Saint Sulpice).

Les Halles (Day #2) has a wide selection of clothing inside the Forum shopping center, or head up nearby Rue du Jour to check out **Agnés B. and Gaultier Junior** for a younger look. There are dozens of other shops on this short street selling new and used clothing for men and women.

Keep an eye out for *Soldes*, seasonal sales that usually take place in January and July. *Liquidation* means "everything must go". Women's and men's clothes are sized from 36 (small) to 48 (extra large). Shoes start at 36 (size 5) through 45 (size 11). Children's clothes are sized by age; baby shoes start at 19. Our advice, of course, is to try things on, and any shop will accommodate this request.

To find everyday items that you need while traveling, whether shampoo, a warm sweater, an insole for your shoe, or a sketch pad for your drawings, try one of the many branches of the **discount department stores** known as **Monoprix, Uniprix** or **Prisunic**. These stores are very handy, located all over town, smaller and less crowded than the major department stores. Most also offer shoe and clothing repair services and have one floor of grocery items. Clean, inexpensive and well-organized, these stores offer good quality merchandise and are pleasant to shop in.

While you can find many **Beauty Care Products** in these stores, smaller specialized boutiques offer more sophisticated products and perfumes as well as services like manicure, hair removal, facial massage etc. in their **Salons de Beauté**. Our favorite is **Magic Beauty**, centrally located at 51 Rue de Rivoli. Call 42.36.06.35 for an appointment, or just stop in – the staff is amiable to walk-ins, a real find in Paris!

Hair Dressers are easy enough to locate, but always busy. One of the most popular salons is **Jacques Dessanges**, with 12 locations in the city. Call the Franklin Roosevelt salon at 43.59.31.31 for information and an appointment. Another favorite is **Jean Louis David**; he has 14 salons and a beauty school with discount prices on modern dos. Call 43.59.82.08. More exclusive is **Maniatis** whose three shops are 18 Rue Marbeuf (Tel: 47.23.30.14) near the Champs-Elysées, 10 Rue Poquelin (Tel: 40.28.90.95) in the Forum des Halles, and 35 Rue de Sévres (Tel: 45.44.16.39) near St. Germain-des-Prés.

Fun souvenirs

The Boutique Chic et Choc in Les Halles Metro station takes the cake. They have all sorts of items with the Paris Metro logo. Another special spot is the **Réunion des Musées Nationaux**, 10 Rue de l'Abbaye, near St. Germain-des-Prés, for posters and catalogues from Paris museums, and scarves, handbags and jewelry inspired by the great collections. Try also the **Louvre des Antiquaires**, 2 Place du Palais Royal, for antique furnishings, prints and paintings. Some of the dealers here have less expensive shops elsewhere, so ask for a card.

Adventurous visitors will head for **Flea Markets** (*marchés aux puces*) to dig out something unique. The most well-known is at the **Porte de Clignancourt**, open during the weekends (Metro: Porte de Clignancourt)). In town, try the **Marché d'Aligre**, a food and flower market which also has a section of old books, clothes, glassware, lace and jewelry (Place d'Aligre, near Bastille, Metro: Ledru-Rollin; closed Monday). Of the markets outside the city, the best for bargains is the **Marché de Montreuil** to the east (Metro: Porte de Montreuil). Old clothes, junk, and genuine finds are here all day Saturday, Sunday and Monday.

A few other suggestions for take-homes that you can pick up and pack easily: perfumed soaps in decorative boxes (look in the pharmacy windows); chocolates and other bonbons in pretty packets, sold in bakeries and *confiseries*, mustard and vinegar assortments in attractive jars and bottles; 'Perfumes of Paris' collections with sample sizes of an assortment of scents, on sale in many of the smaller beauty product boutiques. The only problem with shopping in Paris is trying to decide how much you can spend. But even Uncle Scrooge could spring for a pair of Eiffel Tower earrings (10 to 50 Francs in souvenir shops) or a sachet of lavender to perfume the linen closet (10 to 30 Francs, in department stores or from street vendors).

Calendar of Special Events

The main tourist season in Paris is from June through September, and Easter is also a very busy period. July and August are big holiday months for the French, so a number of shops, restaurants and theaters are closed. However, there is still plenty for visitors to do, including summer festivals, sound and light shows, and fireworks displays, and there is a happy and relaxed atmosphere in the city streets, less crowded than at other times of the year.

From **January through March**, the weather is cold and damp, and the only advantages at this time are the lower fares and hotel rates, and the absence of crowds at museums and monuments.

Springtime in Paris is a legend, of course, and one the city usually lives up to, if for a fleeting moment. Temperatures in **April and May** range from 60 to 70°F (16 to 22°C). The days lengthen deliciously as heavy chestnut blooms appear against the unfurling green foliage. If you are lucky with your timing, Paris in these months is at its most intoxicating. The risk is that you may arrive for a week of rain and

blustery winds, in which case our advice is to visit museums!

In **June and July** there are many celebrations. The Festival du Marais goes on for two months, presenting concerts, theater and dance in some of the neighborhood's lovely old buildings and churches, as well as special events held in major halls. This more than makes up for annual closings. On June 21 is the Fête de la Musique, held on the longest day of the year right into the morning. There are free concerts at outdoor bandstands set up around the city as well as spontaneous events. Every form of music imaginable seems to greet the year on this day.

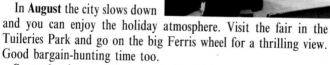

The Tour de France bicycle race sprints to a finish on the Champs-Elysées around July 14. That is Bastille Day, known in France as La Fête Nationale. The party is in the streets, starting with the morning military parade down the Champs-Elysées, through fireworks over the Eiffel Tower, and dancing till dawn at the numerous Firemen's Balls. Watch out for sizzling firecrackers!

In **August** the city slows down and you can enjoy the holiday atmosphere. Visit the fair in the Tuileries Park and go on the big Ferris wheel for a thrilling view. Good bargain-hunting time too.

September is an excellent month for visiting, known as la *rentrée*, or the return. New fashions, plays, and a major art show, the *Foire Internationale de l'Art Contemporain* (F.I.A.C.) liven up the city.

October is wine month, with the Montmartre harvest festival and the arrival of *Beaujolais nouveau*. It is also time for the International Dance Festival, which continues through November.

Christmas starts in the shops around the end of **November**, and the streets are magnificent to see. The days are short and cold, but the city has a bustling, busy quality in the days preceding the end-of-the-year holidays. Christmas is celebrated in the family for the most part, while New Year's Eve is a big party occasion.

National holidays involve bank closings and heavy traffic, so plan around the following: **January 1, Easter Monday, May 1 (Labor Day), May 8 (V.E. Day), Pentecost (Whit Monday), July 14, August 15 (Assumption), November 1 (All Saints' Day), November 11 (Armistice), December 25.**

When packing seasonable clothes for your holiday, keep in mind that the French, and especially Parisians, dress up to go to work, out to dinner, or to the theater. Jeans and sneakers are fine for visiting museums, but frowned upon in many restaurants and shops.

What to Know!
Practical Information

TRAVEL ESSENTIALS

Visas

Travelers to France must have a valid passport. Visitors from EEC countries and America do not need visas, but visitors from other countries should contact the nearest French consulate or tourist office about obtaining one before traveling.

Arrival

You could arrive at one of two airports serving Paris. **Charles de Gaulle** (also referred to as 'Roissy') is bigger and more modern. You can take a comfortable and inexpensive Air France bus to Porte Maillot in the 16th district, then take a bus, the Metro or a cab to your hotel. There are also city buses (N°s 350 and 351) which go into Eastern Paris, Nation and the Gare de l'Est train station. A taxi takes about 40 to 50 minutes to reach the center, and costs about 170 Francs. Add another 30 minutes for rush hours.

Orly is the other major airport, which handles mostly domestic flights and charters. Air France buses go to the Invalides Terminal, a convenient drop-off place, where you can board the Metro or RER directly. A city bus ('Orlybus') comes into the southern end of Paris at the Denfert-Rochereau Metro station every 15 minutes. A taxi ride, not during rush hour, takes 30-40 minutes and costs about 120 Francs.

If you arrive at a train station, you can follow the clearly posted signs towards the Metro or taxi stands.

Time

France is six hours ahead of U.S. Eastern Standard time and two hours ahead of Greenwich Mean Time.

Electricity

Paris runs on 220 volts, 50 cycles, although there are still a few older buildings on 110. Devices marked 220/240 volts will work in Paris, but not at top speed. If you carry a travel iron or hair dryer, for example, make sure you have an adaptor so that it will fit in the French socket. If you've forgotten to bring one along, you can buy one from an 'Electricité' or 'Quincaillerie' (hardware) shop.

GETTING ACQUAINTED

Money

Many banks in Paris will change cash or travelers' checks, and there are no special differences in rates. Banking hours are 9 a.m. to 4.30 p.m. on weekdays. The exchange window at the Gare du Nord is open until 10 p.m. on weekdays, and other station banks are open until 8 p.m.

There are automatic exchange machines at the Opéra (the BNP Bank) and at N° 66 on the Champs-Elysées (BRED) that will convert other bills into Francs. International VISA cards can be used in automatic tellers at many city banks.

If you loose your credit card, here are some hotline numbers: American Express (Tel: 47.77.72.00); Diners Club (Tel: 47.62.75.75); Carte Bleu/Visa (Tel: 42.77.11.90).

The basic unit of money is the Franc, divided into 100 Centimes. Coin units are used for 5, 10, 20 and 50 Centimes; 1, 2, 5 and 10 Francs. In circulation are the bills for 20, 50, 100, 200 and 500 Francs.

At the time of publication, the exchange rate is about 4.8 Francs to a U.S. Dollar and 9.5 Francs to one Pound Sterling. Of course you'll have to check the rate before you go, and keep your eye on it during the trip!

A few sample costs in Paris: Movie tickets 30-50 Francs; theater 80+ Francs; glass of wine in a café 10-15 Francs; soft drink 10+ Francs; tea 18 Francs; pastry in a bakery 10-15 Francs; pastry in a café 20-30 Francs; cigarettes 10-15 Francs a pack; foreign newspapers 8+ Francs.

Tipping

Common in a number of situations; in hotels, restaurants and cafés, service charge is always included. However, people usually leave something in the saucer, often the small change returned from the bill. Prices may be listed *prix nets* or *service compris*, in which case, service is included in the price. If the price says *service en sus* or *service non compris*, you can expect an extra 12 or 15 percent to be added to the total.

A tip of 2 Francs is usually given to: room service waiters (except breakfast), ushers, washroom attendants, hat check clerks. Taxi drivers and hairdressers expect about 15%.

GETTING AROUND

Paris is divided into 20 *arrondissements* (districts) which spiral out from the Louvre Palace in a small-shell pattern. The last numbers of the postal code beginning with 750- are the *arrondissement* numbers. Handy book-format street maps are on sale in most *café-tabacs*, news stands and many bookstores. While in the Metro, ask for a free map (*un plan du Métro*) and a copy of the public transportation guide 'Paris Patchwork'.

You can travel on **bus and Metro** with tickets purchased at the ticket booth in any Metro station, much cheaper (34.5 Francs) when you buy ten at once (*un carnet*). There is a tourist card called **Paris Visite**, valid for three to five days (80 or 130 Francs) of unlimited travel on the Metro, bus (in-

Gare St. Lazare

cluding airports), and suburban SNCF lines.

The one-day card is called **Formule 1**. The first gives discounts on certain boat tours, the Montparnasse Tower, and SNCF bicycle rental at Compiègne or Vernon (among other stations).

It is very simple to use the **Metro** system, which is the densest in the world with stops an average of every 55 meters. The lines are named for their terminal points, for example Château de Vincennes-Pont de Neuilly crosses the city from east to west, ending at those two stops. You can transfer as many times as you need to on the same ticket, by following the orange signs marked *Correspondances* in the tunnels.

There are big maps in every station to guide you. In general, the Metro is quite safe, although you must watch out for your wallet; especially when in big crowds.

Trains run from 5.30 a.m. to 12.30 a.m. every day. Follow the sign *Accès aux Quais* to reach the tracks, and *Sortie* to get out to the street. Keep a hold of your ticket until you exit, it may be checked by inspectors.

Buses run on different schedules, but

usually start around 7 a.m. and stop around 8.45 p.m., only certain buses run on Sunday or late at night. Bus shelters all have maps and route information, and if you board a bus you must show your pass or punch a ticket in the machine next to the driver. Look at the route map to see how many bus zones you'll be going through, if more than two, you must punch two tickets; except for the Petite Ceinture, a bus service which circles the boundaries of Paris. You would need to use up to five tickets to complete the round.

If you're good at deciphering public transportation systems, the city buses are really a great way to get around, even though they are admittedly not as fast as the Metro.

The RER lines are rapid transit lines that go out to the suburbs. They can be useful for crossing town quickly, and you can use a Metro ticket within the city. But to get to Versailles, for example, if you don't have a pass that covers it, you must buy a more expensive ticket, which you will have to insert in a machine in order to exit the station on arrival.

Taxis are best found at taxi stands, clearly marked by large signs. You can also call a taxi company. Alpha Taxi (Tel: 45.85.85.85); Taxi Bleu: (Tel: 42.02.42.02). Both offer 24-hour service. If you call a taxi, the meter starts running when the driver gets the call.

There is an extra charge for luggage, train-station pick-up, and sometimes authorized rate hikes may be posted in the window. Three passengers is the limit, and cabbies are strict about this particular rule.

We do not recommend renting a car to visit Paris. Driving conditions are difficult and you really have no need of suffering traffic jams.

Banks have various hours (see travel information, "Money"), generally from 9 a.m. to 4.30 p.m. Monday through Friday, with some branches closed at lunchtime, and/or on Monday and some open on Saturday until noon.

The **Post Office** is open daily from 9 a.m. to 6 p.m. and Saturday until noon (for branches with longer hours, see Mail and Telephone in this chapter.)

Department stores are open from 10 a.m. to 6.30 p.m., and normally close on Sunday. Many smaller shops close on Monday (especially food stores) and some on Wednesday. Bakeries and some others close for lunch for various lengths of time from about 1 p.m. to 4 p.m. Most shops open until 7 or 8 p.m.

Public offices are open from 9 a.m. to 5 p.m. Monday to Friday, and sometimes on Saturday morning, often closed for two hours from 12 to 2 p.m.

MAIL AND TELEPHONE

Post offices are open from 8 a.m. to 6 p.m. Monday through Friday, and some are open until noon on Saturday. You can spot them by the yellow sign

with a bird silhouette and the letters "PTT". There are two branches with extended hours. **Poste du Louvre** (52 Rue du Louvre, 75001, Metro: Louvre or Les Halles); 8 a.m. to midnight Sunday through Thursday and 24 hours on Friday, Saturday and the 14th and 15th of each month. **Poste Paris 8** (71 Ave. des Champs-Elysées, 75008, Metro: Franklin Roosevelt), which are open from 8 a.m. to 11 p.m., Monday through Friday.

Public telephones can be found in all post offices; there are booths on the street; a *café-tabac* has a telephone and most ordinary cafés have phones for the use of customers. In cafés, you may have to buy a token (*jeton*) at the counter, or pay the cashier directly, or use a coin in the phone. Otherwise, most public phones now take *Télécartes*, plastic cards. You can buy 50 *unités* (calling units) for 40 Francs, or 120 for 96 Francs. They are useful for local and international calls; a flashing panel tells you how much time you have left.

To make a **Collect or Credit Card Call**, dial 19, wait for the tone, dial 33 followed by the country code to reach the operator. To dial other countries first dial the international access code 19, wait for the second bleep, then the relevant country code: Australia (61); Germany (49); Italy (39); Japan (81); Netherlands (31); Spain (34); UK (44); US and Canada (1). If you are using a US credit phone card, dial the company's access number below – Sprint, Tel: 19 0087; AT&T, Tel: 19 0011; MCI, Tel: 19 00 19.

Telegrams can be sent from any Post Office. There is a special phone number for telegrams in English: 42.33.21.11. **Telefax** services are available at the Louvre Post Office (address above) and at a few branches. There is a Telex service at 7 Rue Feydeau (75002), open from 8 a.m. to 8 p.m., Metro: Bourse.

WHERE TO STAY

Although there are many, many hotels in Paris, due to the steady stream of visitors – not just seasonal tourists but also visitors to trade fairs, congresses and the like – it can be hard to find a room. Your travel agent will probably offer to book a room for you, which is a good idea. Otherwise, it is wise to reserve in advance. If you haven't done so, you can save foot-work by checking with the Tourist Office on the Champs-Elysées (Metro: Charles De Gaulle) or in any of the train stations. They charge a small fee for finding a room. You can

also call or write to the hotels listed below to make a reservation. In that case, be prepared to send a deposit ahead of you. Your choice ranges from the deluxe to the merely adequate. Here are a few suggestions at different rates. Breakfast is usually extra, starting at about 40 Francs for a continental breakfast.

Deluxe Hotels

A double room with a bath costs between 1,800 and 2,500 Francs a night in these establishments.

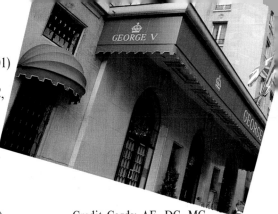

Inter-Continental-Paris
3 Rue de Castiglione (75001)
Tel: 44.77.11.19
Credit Cards: AE, DC, MC, VISA.
460 rooms, excellent location, great service, all modern conveniences including air conditioning.

Meurice
228 Rue de Rivoli (75001)
Tel: 42.60.38.60
Credit Cards: AE, DC, MC, VISA.
161 rooms, modern conveniences in a lovely old building, air conditioning.

Ritz
15 Place Vendôme (75001)
Tel: 42.60.38.30
Credit Cards: AE, DC, MC, VISA.
Everything is perfect. This hotel was the inspiration for the word 'ritzy'. 164 rooms, good restaurants, spacious public rooms, all conveniences, air conditioning and secretarial services.

Crillon
10 Place de la Concorde (75008)
Tel: 42.65.24.24
Credit Cards: AE, DC, MC, VISA.
191 rooms, fantastic site with some views over the river, next door to the American Embassy. Completely refurbished in the early 1980s, excellent restaurant, air conditioning.

Plaza-Athénée
25 Ave. Montaigne (75008)
Tel: 47.23.78.33
Credit Cards: AE, DC, MC, VISA.
218 sound-proofed rooms and suites near the Champs-Elysées. Restaurants, disco, air conditioning.

George V
31 Ave. George V (75008)
Tel: 47.23.54.00
Credit Cards: AE, DC, MC, VISA.
292 rooms, completely modern and air-conditioned. The restaurant and bar are very popular with the international upper-crust, including starlets, film agents and businessmen.

Expensive hotels

For a double room with a bath, expect to pay about 600 to 900 Francs.

Normandy
7 Rue de l'Echelle (75001)
Tel: 42.60.30.21
Credit Cards: AE, DC, MC, VISA.
138 rooms, most with bathrooms. Restaurant and bar. Comfortable and relaxing.

Deux-Iles
59 Rue St. Louis-en-L'Ile (75004)
Tel: 43.26.13.35
17 rooms, all with bath or shower in a lovely 17th-century house; peaceful and friendly; bar and sitting room.

Angleterre
44 Rue Jacob (75006)
Tel: 42.60.34.72
Credit Cards: AE, DC, VISA.
30 rooms, all with bath or shower, in what was once the home of the British Ambassador. Good service, traditional surroundings, central location.

Régina

2 Place des Pyramides (75001)
Tel: 42.60.31.10
Credit Cards: AE, DC, VISA.
Numerous films have been shot in this elegant hotel which is centrally situated with a view of the Tuileries. Prices of rooms vary between 750 and 1,600 Francs so do check when booking.

Terrass

12-14 Rue Joseph-de-Maistre (75018)
Tel: 46.06.72.85
Credit Cards: AE, DC, MC, VISA.
108 rooms in Montmartre, baths. Restaurant and bar, situated in a calm location.

Moderate hotels

One night in a double hotel room of this category costs about 250 to 500 Francs. All of the below have fewer than 100 rooms, some with bath/shower rooms and some without.

Timhôtel

This new, moderately priced chain has several hotels in town, all well-outfitted (all rooms with bath) and small and friendly. All are recommended highly and definitely require reservations. Here are their locations:

Italie

22 Rue Barrault (75013)

Tolbiac

35 Rue Tolbiac (75013)

Montmartre

11 Place Emile Goudeau (75018)

Le Louvre

4 Rue Croix des Petits Champs (75001)

La Bourse

3 Rue de la Banque (75002)

Saint Lazare

113 Rue St. Lazare (75008)

*For all the Timhôtels listed above, call the central reservation service to book a room:*Tel: **42.96.28.28**
Credit Cards: AE, DC, MC, VISA

Grandes Ecoles

75 Rue du Cardinal Lemoine (75005)
Tel: 43.26.79.23
Not very fancy, but well-located and pleasant, good value.

St. Jacques

35 Rue des Ecoles (75005)
Tel: 43.26.82.53
Like the above, an ordinary Parisian hotel, centrally located.

Bastille Speria

1 Rue Bastille (75004)
Tel: 42.72.04.01
Credit Cards: AE, DC, VISA.
An old building which was totally refurbished in 1988. Rooms small but quiet.

Inexpensive hotels

This hard-to-find category includes hotels between 230 and 350 Francs. The rooms provide minimal but adequatecomfort. There may be a big difference in price between rooms with and without private bath/shower/toilet.

Palais

2 Quai de la Mégisserie (75001)
Tel: 42.36.98.25
19 rooms near the Sainte Chapelle, some with bathrooms.

Esmeralda
4 Rue St. Julien le Pauvre (75002)
Tel: 43.54.19.20
19 rooms (16 with bath/shower rooms) near Notre Dame in the busy Latin Quarter.

Castex Hotel
5 Rue Castex (75004)
Tel: 42.72.31.31
A small but very well run family hotel which is located close to the Bastille. Guests are advised to book from Easter onwards.

Nevers-Luxembourg
3 Rue Abbé-de-l'Epée (75005)
Tel: 43.26.81.83
26 rooms, 8 with bath or shower rooms, attractive and good value.

Vieux Paris
9 Rue Gît-le-Coeur (75006)
Tel: 43.54.41.66
21 rooms, 14 with bath or showers, near the river and St. Michel. Quaint, albeit slightly frayed furnishings.

Palais Bourbon
49 Rue de Bourgogne (75007)
Tel: 47.05.29.26
26 rooms with bath/shower and 8 others without. Small but modern, has a bar. Quiet, distinguished neighborhood of government ministries, the Invalides and the Rodin Museum.

HEALTH AND EMERGENCIES

If you lose your money, passport or other papers, or if they are stolen, look for the police station (*Commissariat*) nearest the site of theft or loss to make an official declaration before reporting to the embassy of your country.

Police Emergency
Tel: 17

Fire Department
Tel: 18 (emergency first aid)

Doctor
SOS Médecins
Tel: 43.37.77.77 or 47.07.77.77

American Hospital
Tel: 47.47.53.00.

British Hospital
Tel: 47.58.13.12

British and American Pharmacy
1 Rue Auber (75009)
Metro: Opéra.
Mon-Sat. 8.30 a.m. to 8 p.m.
English spoken.

Pharmacie Anglo-Américaine
6 Rue Castiglione (75001)
Metro: Tuileries.
Mon.-Sat. 9 a.m. to 7.30 p.m.
English spoken.

SOS-Help
English language.
Crisis hot line: 42.93.31.31 from 3 p.m. to 11 p.m. (subject to change).

The museums of Paris deserve every bit of the praise lavished upon them by visitors from near and far. Check the *Officiel* magazine for ongoing exhibitions and precise information on opening hours (these are subject to change). City of Paris museums close on Monday, national museums on Tuesday, and private museums may close on Tuesday or Friday. Admission charges vary, but 40 Francs is about the maximum for one adult entrance. There are reductions for students, children under 18, and seniors, so bring along identification if you fit any of these categories. Many national museums are free or half-priced on Sunday. The **Carte Musées** (available in main Metro stations, museums and monuments) gives you access to over 60 museums and monuments in Paris (including the Louvre, Orsay, Pompidou, Picasso, La Vilette, Versailles, Notre Dame…) for a period of 1, 3 or 5 days.

In addition to the museums included in the itineraries in this book, there are many others well worth a visit. Here are a few:

Musée d'Orsay
1 Rue de Bellechasse (75007)
Metro: Solférino; RER: Orsay
Open from 10 a.m. to 6 p.m., Thursday until 9.15 p.m. (tickets sold until 8). Closed on Tuesday.

The vast, long-abandoned Orsay train station in the center of town was saved from destruction many years ago, but not until recently did it discover its new vocation.

Preserving the building's *belle époque* architecture, Gae Aulenti redesigned the inner space into several exhibition levels, while keeping all the open, airy majesty of the original train station.

Now it is devoted to works from the last half of the 19th century. One section, showing works by Delacroix and Ingres, leads up to the birth of impressionism in the 1870s. Witness the changing aesthetics in works by Monet, Manet and Renoir. On the upper level, there are numerous works by Van Gogh and Cézanne. A good part of the collection is from the old *Jeu de Paume Museum* (now completely closed down).

Exhibitions in the two towers bring us up to the end of the century with sleek Art Nouveau. Between them, a platform and a giant transparent clock provide a pretty view across the Seine river to the gardens of the Louvre. You can rest and refresh yourself at the restaurant/café on this level.

Musée des Arts Décoratifs
107-109 Rue de Rivoli (75001)
Metro: Palais Royal
Open 12.30 p.m. to 6 p.m. Closed on Monday and Tuesday.

This recently renovated museum is heaven for interior decorators. Beautifully crafted furniture, shiny porcelain and crystal, gleaming silver and gold objects as well as statues and paintings are on exhibit.

Musée d'Orsay

Musée d'Art Moderne de la Ville de Paris
11 Ave. du President Wilson (75016)
Metro: Alma-Marceau, Iéna.
Open 10 a.m. to 5 p.m., Wednesday until 8.30 p.m. Closed on Monday.

Somewhat neglected, overshadowed

by many other new museums in recent years, this big, echoing place is usually calm, cool and uncrowded on a summer day, a good place to seek relief from the crowds and the elements. The period of art represented here falls somewhere between Orsay and the Pompidou Center, Post Impressionism up through Braque and Rouault. One wing now houses the **Musée d'Art et d'Essai** (closed on Tuesday). Also known as the *Palais de Tokyo*, the space is used for changing exhibits.

Musée Grévin (Waxworks)

10 Blvd. Montmartre (75009) and 'Grand Balcon' in the Forum des Halles shopping center.

The first (Metro: Rue Montmartre) is open daily from 1 p.m. to 7 p.m. (last tickets sold at 6). The second (Metro: Les Halles) is open from 10.20 a.m. to 7.30 p.m. on weekdays, and from 1 p.m. to 8 p.m. on Sunday and holidays. Plenty of turn-of-the-century characters and a few present-day stars animate the museums, which are very popular with children.

SPECIAL SERVICES

For children, there are several baby-sitting services available in town; we recommend **Kid Service** (Tel: 42.66.00.52). Museums that are specially interesting to young travelers are Orsay (interactive computer terminals), Musée de la Marine, La Villette. There is a very good children's library in the Pompidou Center, where older kids can amuse themselves while big folks tour the museum. Kids old enough can also be left in the Jardin des Halles play area at the Forum des Halles while you shop. There are puppet theaters in the Luxembourg Gardens, in the Champs de Mars park next to the Eiffel Tower, and at

the Rond Point des Champs-Elysées in the middle of the Avenue.

Students must bring a valid student I.D. with a photo in order to get reductions at museums, movies, theaters, and for concerts. You can get more information on what's available at the Council on International Educational Exchange, 1 Place de l'Odéon (75006).

Another useful address for young travelers is the *Accueil des Jeunes en France*, 119 Rue St. Martin (75004), Metro: Rambuteau. They can help with budget lodging and information on activities where you can meet people.

Handicapped Travelers will have difficulty using public transportation and access to many older buildings is limited. Some efforts are made however, and there is a taxi service for people in wheelchairs, special bus service for the disabled, and the Louvre museum offers tours for handicapped (including blind) individuals. The government publishes a booklet, *Touristes quand même*, which you can order or pick up at the French National Tourist Office, Parisian tourist offices, or directly from the *Comité National Français de Liason pour la Réadaptation des Handicapés*, 38 Blvd. Raspail (75007).

Seniors in Paris can benefit from many reductions and advantages after age 60 or 65. In order to do so, you of course must provide proof of age, and in some cases (for reduced train fare, for example) you will have to provide a passport-sized photo which is affixed to a discount card.

A reduction for families together (*Familles nombreuses*) is applied in some museums and for train fares at off-peak periods.

FURTHER INFORMATION

The **main Tourist Office** for Paris is at 127 Avenue des Champs-Elysées (75008), Metro: Charles de Gaulle-Etoile. It is often crowded, but the staff does a good job providing information in English, booking hotels or travel arrangements, and distributing maps and brochures. There are branches in train stations and airports as well. The phone number for tourist information in English is: 47.20.88.98.

The *Agence Nationale pour l'Information Touristique* will send you information by mail if you write to them at 8 Avenue de l'Opéra (75001). Of course, you can also contact the French Government Tourist Office in your own country.

To keep on top of what is happening while you are in town, the *Official des Spectacles* is an invaluable aid. A small magazine priced at two Francs, it publishes an extensive list of restaurants, bars and clubs, concerts, plays and movies in town, information on museums, tours and sports, with hours, addresses and phone numbers. Similar and equally good magazines are *Sept à Paris* and *Pariscope*.

In English, *Passion* magazine is a big-format monthly with restaurant and film reviews, calendar of events,

and a summer supplement mini-guide. You can find these three publications at any newsstand.

American and British papers and magazines are available at many newsstands too. For further English reading, try these big bookshops:

Brentano's
37 Ave. de l'Opéra (75002)
Metro: *Opéra*

Galignani
224 Rue de Rivoli (75001)
Metro: *Tuileries*

Shakespeare & Co.
37 Rue de la Bûcherie (75005)
Metro: *St. Michel*

W.H. Smith
248 Rue de Rivoli (75001)
Metro: *Concorde.*

EMBASSIES

Australia
4 Rue Jean-Rey (75015)
Metro: *Bir Hakeim*
Tel: 40.59.33.00
Mon.-Fri. 9 a.m. to 5.30 p.m.

Canada
(Embassy and Consulate)
35 Ave. Montaigne (75008)
Metro: *Franklin Roosevelt or Alma Marceau.*
Tel: 47.23.01.01.
Mon.-Fri. 9 a.m. to 4.30 p.m.

Denmark
77 Ave. Marceau (75016)
Tel: 47.20.32.66

Egypt
56 Ave. Iéna (75016)
Tel: 47.20.97.70

Finland
39 Quay d'Orsay (75007)
Tel: 47.05.35.45

Hungary
5 bis Sq. Ave. Foche (75016)
Tel: 45.00.41.59

India
15 Rue Alfred Dehodencq (75016)
Tel: 45.20.39.30

Ireland
4 Rue Rude (75016)
Tel: 45.00.20.87

Israel
3 Rue Rabelais (75008)
Tel: 42.56.47.47

Japan
7 Ave. Hoche (75008)
Tel: 47.66.02.22

Kuwait
2 Rue Lubek (75016)
Tel: 47.23.54.25

Malaysia
32 Rue Spontini (75016)
Tel: 45.53.11.85

Netherlands
7 Rue Eibie (75007)
Tel: 43.06.61.88

New Zealand
Embassy and Consulate)
7 Rue Léonard-da-Vinci (75016)
Metro: Victor Hugo.
Tel: 45.00.24.11

Norway
28 Rue Bayard (75008)
Tel: 47.23.72.78

Pakistan
18 Rue Lord Byron (75008)
Tel: 45.62.23.32

Philippines
39 Ave. Georges Mandel (75016)
Tel: 47.04.65.50

Qatar
57 Quai Orsay (75007)
Tel: 45.51.90.71

Saudi Arabia
5 Ave. Hoche (75008)
Tel: 47.66.00.13

Singapore
12 Sq. Ave. Foch (75016)
Tel: 45.00.33.61

Sweden
17 Rue Barbet de Jouy (75007)
Tel: 45.55.92.15

U.A.E.
3 Rue Lotta (75016)
Tel: 45.53.94.04

United Kingdom
(Embassy) 35 Rue Fbg. St. Honoré
(75008)
(Consulate) 2 Rue d'Anjou (75008)
Metro: Concorde or Madeleine.
Tel: 42.66.91.42
Mon.-Fri. 9.30 a.m. to 5.30 p.m.

United States of America
(Embassy) 2 Avenue Gabriel
(75008)
(Consulate) 2 Rue St. Florentin
(75001)
Tel: 42.96.12.02. Metro: Concorde.
Mon.-Fri. 9 a.m. to 6 p.m.

U.S.S.R.
79 Rue de Grenelle (75007)
Tel: 45.48.99.28

Index

NOTES

INSIGHT GUIDES

COLORSET NUMBERS

You'll find the colorset number on the spine of each Insight Guide.

INSIGHT *pocket* GUIDES

EXISTING & FORTHCOMING TITLES:

United States: Houghton Mifflin Company, Boston MA 02108
Tel: (800) 2253362 Fax: (800) 4589501

Canada: Thomas Allen & Son, 390 Steelcase Road East
Markham, Ontario L3R 1G2
Tel: (416) 4759126 Fax: (416) 4756747

Great Britain: GeoCenter UK, Hampshire RG22 4BJ
Tel: (256) 817987 Fax: (256) 817988

Worldwide: Höfer Communications Singapore 2262
Tel: (65) 8612755 Fax: (65) 8616438

66 I was first drawn to the Insight Guides by the excellent "Nepal" volume. I can think of no book which so effectively captures the essence of a country. Out of these pages leaped the Nepal I know – the captivating charm of a people and their culture. I've since discovered and enjoyed the entire Insight Guide Series. Each volume deals with a country or city in the same sensitive depth, which is nowhere more evident than in the superb photography. 99

Sir Edmund Hillary

NOTES